HOUSING, 'RACE', SOCIAL POLICY AND EMPOWERMENT

Research in Ethnic Relations Series

Race, Discourse and Power in France
Maxim Silverman

Paradoxes of Multiculturalism
Essays on Swedish Society
Aleksandra Ålund and Carl-Ulrik Schierup

Ethnicity, Class, Gender and Migration
Greek-Cypriots in Britain
Floya Anthias

The Migration Process in Britain and West Germany
Two Demographic Studies of Migrant Populations
Heather Booth

Perceptions of Israeli Arabs: Territoriality and Identity
Izhak Schnell

Ethnic Mobilisation in a Multi-cultural Europe
Edited by John Rex and Beatrice Drury

Post-war Caribbean Migration to Britain:
The Unfinished Cycle
Margaret Byron

Through Different Eyes: The Cultural Identity
of Young Chinese People in Britain
David Parker

Britannia's Crescent: Making a Place for Muslims
in British Society
Danièle Joly

Housing, 'Race', Social Policy and Empowerment

M.L. HARRISON
'Race' and Public Policy Research Unit
School of Sociology and Social Policy
University of Leeds

Avebury

Aldershot • Brookfield USA • Hong Kong • Singapore • Sydney

Published by
Avebury
Ashgate Publishing Limited
Gower House
Croft Road
Aldershot
Hants GU11 3HR
England

Ashgate Publishing Company
Old Post Road
Brookfield
Vermont 05036
USA

British Library Cataloguing in Publication Data

Harrison, M.L.
  Housing, 'Race', Social Policy and
  Empowerment. - (Research in Ethnic
  Relations Series)
  I. Title II. Series
  362.84

ISBN 1 85628 860 9

Library of Congress Catalog Card Number: 95-77878

Typeset by
Ashville Secretarial & Business Services
7 Ashville Terrace
New Street, Farley
Leeds, LS28 5AT
Printed in Great Britain by Ipswich Book Co. Ltd., Ipswich, Suffolk.

Contents

Preface

The term empowerment has been appearing increasingly frequently in the literature of social welfare, and in the world of housing practice. It seems to be something generally approved of, but hard to agree on in terms of a universal definition or an agenda. This book developed out of an interest in specific instances or aspects of empowerment, as observed in relation to housing. The writer moved from empirical investigations - covering black run housing organizations, mainstream associations, and relationships with building firms - to issues of choice and theory of a wider kind. In a sense the book is about interactions between agency and structure, since it deals with the context in which social welfare movements operate, the differentiated nature of social policy, and the strategies which minority ethnic groups and individuals have pursued. It is also about understanding the welfare state.

Thanks are due to the many scholars and practitioners who have given advice or support. As chapters have taken shape a number of people within Leeds University have commented on the arguments and material, or provided information. Amongst these generous colleagues have been Ian Law, Kirk Mann, Deborah Phillips, and Alison Ravetz. The responsibility for errors and misinterpretations in the book, however, of course remains mine. From the world of practice Elaine Bowes, Cathy Davis, Louis Julienne, and Arun Misra stand out for their support and encouragement. At the same time there have been numerous others who have helped with information, comment and understanding over the last six years.

Nowadays much academic work in UK social science has a hasty character, because day to day pressures make it so hard to sustain standards in research and writing. For this book the author has needed to compromise in order to complete the task, and hopes that readers will forgive any consequent lapses in scholarship. As far as investigations in the field were concerned, however, support from charitable sources made possible some successful surveys and case studies. The Wingate and Rowntree Foundations provided resources without which the fieldwork would have been impossible. Finally, thanks are due to Jacqui Davies, who carried out a large share of the research on the contractors project referred to in chapter 6. Preparation of the manuscript has been handled by Ashville Secretarial and Business Services, with efficiency and understanding.

List of abbreviations

ATSIC	Aboriginal and Torres Strait Islander Commission
BCA	The Black Contractors Association
BICBUS	Birmingham Inner City Builders Support Unit
CRE	Commission for Racial Equality
FBHO	Federation of Black Housing Organisations
JRF	Joseph Rowntree Foundation
LEOF	London Equal Opportunities Federation
NFHA	National Federation of Housing Associations
WAMT	Women and Manual Trades

1 Introduction

This book deals with housing, but also touches on questions about 'race' relations, community empowerment, and the development of social policies. Although several chapters are heavily empirical, some include comment on more philosophical or theoretical issues. The agenda has come from two concerns. On the one hand was a wish to combine, interpret and present some recent research material on housing practices, struggles and outcomes in the area of ethnic or 'race' relations. On the other was the intention that analysis of housing issues should be related to wider questions in social policy and social theory, and if possible help inform - albeit modestly - our general understanding of the welfare state in the 1980s and 1990s. Many old certainties about welfare systems seem to have dissolved in recent decades; at least that is an impression obtained by observing the privatization of services or the recent rhetoric of consumer sovereignty, choice and pluralism. At the same time the challenges of urban disadvantage, racism and ethnic diversity have pressed more and more forcefully on the public agenda. This book comments on the present character of the UK welfare state, looks into some aspects of conditions and change from housing and 'race' perspectives, and tries to review the implications that certain events in urban housing might have for our view of welfare state restructuring. As we shall see, despite many changes, some of the preoccupations of the past - about inequalities in power or resources, and about the relevance of universalistic arrangements - are by no means obsolete concerns.

The basis and goals for the book

At the heart of the empirical coverage in this book is research material gathered between 1989 and 1994 on housing associations, Britain's black voluntary housing movement, and ethnic minority building contractors. As stated in the preface, thanks are due to the charitable foundations that funded most of the field work and surveys, and to practitioners and scholars (here and abroad) who have given assistance. Chapter 6 also owes a great deal to excellent interviewing and related work carried out by Jacqui Davies in 1993/94.

The programme of research projects drawn upon for chapters 5 and 6 explored what were then relatively under-researched topics, where few data had previously been available. As well as gathering new material, the present author was also able to consider - in highly specific contexts - issues of community empowerment, incorporation and separatism, which had been under-emphasized in housing literature. These issues seemed potentially important not only for housing, but for the wider study of social policy in an apparently increasingly pluralistic era. At the same time there was the hope of making connections with earlier work on the welfare state and social divisions. The result is a book that attempts to offer something on several distinct intellectual fronts. In summary, we are trying to provide coverage in four ways:-

1. For housing specialists and students there is an introduction to current 'race' and housing issues, and an account of some significant features of the social housing scene. There are also some ideas on linking regular day to day housing concerns with broader questions about politics and social change.

2. For theorists of the welfare state there is case study material and argument that may be of interest. No overarching theoretical position or normative standpoint is put forward, but the work is driven by the belief that detailed analysis of public policy topics and collective actions can generate ideas helpful for theory building.

3. For students of 'race' or racism there is a perspective which stresses the importance and pervasiveness of the institutions of the state, and highlights the relevance of collective political action as well as individual strategies in social policy contexts.

4. For practitioners and activists who favour greater equality of opportunities, there is some information in this book about current issues, prospects and obstacles.

The present chapter makes some preliminary points about relating housing studies to social policy concerns, explains the limitations of the book, and outlines the content and key arguments of the chapters that follow. There is then a brief guide to the way in which terminology is used in subsequent chapters.

Housing studies, 'race' and social policy

As this book seeks to cross academic boundaries, some comment is needed on the previous record of writings, and on the desirability of linking up housing, 'race' and social policy. Areas of social policy are often studied by scholars who specialize in a particular field. This is certainly true for housing, where there is a strong tradition of skilled and detailed research looking at physical and social conditions and the workings of specific laws and agencies. It is easy for students to find good collections or texts focussed around the complexities of housing policies, their consequences, or their implementation. Well known recent examples from this housing studies tradition include Malpass and Murie (1994), Malpass and Means (1993), or Cole and Furbey (1994). The tasks facing housing researchers or teachers in their own subject area, however, are often so time-consuming that it can prove difficult to build bridges with broader developments or ideas outside the housing mainstream. Given the pressures to specialize - in the UK at least - too few mainstream housing writers have had the chance to tackle detailed housing issues by placing them in relation to broad developments in social policy, welfare state theory, or features of social change.

Fortunately there are exceptions. Students can obtain a good impression of general housing/social policy/social services links from two leading texts (Spicker, 1989; Clapham, Kemp and Smith, 1990), while there is a scatter of other similarly orientated material across monographs, edited collections, journals, etc. A few scholars have explicitly linked housing with general social theory analyses (for instance Kemeny, 1992). Beyond this there are certain more specific topics where writers on housing have given substantial accounts well connected with social theorizing, analyses of state activity or issues of stratification. This applies notably for owner occupation, for gender divisions, and for racism (see for example Saunders, 1990; Forrest, Murie and Williams, 1990; Rex and Moore, 1967; Smith, 1989). Indeed the debates on 'race' and 'housing classes', and on the social and political implications of owner occupation, have been influences in the development of ideas about stratification, managerialism, and the politics of sectoral or urban consumption cleavages (see for instance discussions in Dunleavy, 1980; Saunders, 1990; Savage, Barlow, Dickens and Fielding, 1992).

Nonetheless, despite major contributions made on the boundary between housing and social theories, there remain important gaps in the literature. In particular, few recent housing books have drawn on the rich detail of housing experiences and practices to inform and move forward more general debates about welfare, power, and political change. One hope of the present volume is to highlight some possible avenues for doing this in relation to selected themes in the study of social policy. These themes are *community empowerment*, *pluralism, incorporation/marginalisation, universalism/selectivity,* and *the role of social welfare movements*. At the same time the intention is indirectly to reassert the importance of analyses which are institutionally orientated, both for the study of social welfare and in academic work on 'race' and ethnic relations. To understand the operation of racism in social policy one needs to take account of how the welfare state is structured, and the general character and impact of its institutions. This may require not only an awareness of some kinds of theories, but also attention to detailed events and situations, such as those in the housing sphere. We should take a cautious view of theory created 'top down', from above, without detailed knowledge of specific instances, histories and struggles. Parallel with this need to continue to inform studies of 'race' by an institutional analysis that goes beyond 'race', there is also the need to inform welfare state theories through a constant assertion of the significance of the ethnic dimension for understanding welfare. Housing scholars have provided a stream of case study material over the years which has helped to illuminate the workings of racism in the welfare state (see chapter 4). General theories of welfare systems need to accommodate and account for such findings.

The limitations of this study

The agenda introduced above may sound very ambitious, so it may be as well to declare the book's limitations at the outset. First, most of the empirical material is drawn from the UK, and comparative treatment of issues is therefore restricted.[1] While several of the broader themes dealt with are relevant in many 'advanced' industrial societies, the detailing usually comes from UK experience. Second, the volume does not attempt to sketch, justify, review or insert a 'grand theory' about society or political economy, critical, normative or otherwise. An aim is to raise issues that may be relevant to broad theorizing, but there will be no attempt to borrow a comprehensive analysis from the current fashion book of social science, or to create a new model at a grand level. Readers will *not* find coverage of the large (and frequently helpful) social movements literature in this volume, nor will much space be devoted to trends in abstract theorizing about the impact of postfordism or so-called 'postmodernism', or the supposed merits of regulation theory. Instead the hope is to set discussion at a fairly unpretentious level, so that student or scholar can read the book without needing much prior knowledge of neo-Marxist debate, 'new right' philosophies, or any elaborate body of received wisdom about social, political, or economic relationships. Where theory is discussed it is more likely to be of a 'middle range' kind, somewhat below the level of the ambitious modelling which inevitably characterizes analyses of the broad economy, polity or state. It is at this middle

4

level that detailed empirical material becomes so valuable. The author's own standpoint and assumptions, however, are made clear wherever possible. In particular, the book carries a preference for the idea that state agencies in many countries are likely to be heavily engaged in the management and organization of household consumption (and related employment), and that a politics of differentiation, incorporation and exclusion has developed around this process (as well as helping to shape it). Some of the research drawn on in this book was influenced from the start by this belief (although the writer tried to keep criticisms and alternative arguments in view at the same time).

The contents of the chapters in outline

Chapters 2 and 3 contain general scene setting material, mainly about inequalities, structures, empowerment, and urban policies in the welfare state. Chapter 4 outlines the experiences and conditions of minority ethnic groups, primarily from a housing research perspective. Chapters 5 and 6 present some information on social housing, the UK's black voluntary housing movement, and housing association investment in relation to community development, referring extensively to research carried out from Leeds University. Chapter 7 tackles some issues of politics and social policy, considering general lessons from the material and findings in earlier chapters, and puts forward ideas about mobilization, empowerment and particularism. Finally, the last chapter draws together what has been said in the different parts of the book, and discusses some options for the future of social policy in complex urban societies.

A sketch of the key arguments and themes of the book

Given the wide variety of issues dealt with, there are several interrelated themes, lines of argument, and topics covered in the different chapters. These will be introduced now in a summarized form, under five headings.

Welfare divisions, organized consumption and empowerment

In a society where stratification and differentiation have been subjected to so much analysis and debate - as in the UK - plenty of explanations and accounts may be on offer dealing with issues of poverty and inequality. Alongside longstanding notions about class relationships being the cause, we are offered newer social theories about gender, disability and racism. Chapter 2 notes that in many settings processes of relative deprivation and exclusion operate, to diminish or constrict the lives of some groups, while others prosper. Characteristically it is disabled people, certain minority ethnic households, and many households headed by women that fare worst, not merely via the operation of inherited wealth or discrimination in private markets, but also - apparently - through the activities of 'the state' itself. This has been illuminated over several decades by social scientists, with the 'Social Division of Welfare' thesis proving one valuable starting point for analysis. One implication is that to some extent there might be connections between marginalisation in the world of mainstream politics and disadvantage in the operation of social and economic practices and policies. For black people or disabled people, for example, representation through mainstream electoral channels has been poor, while the welfare state has made only a limited impact on reducing their relative disadvantages. It is not implausible to suggest that greater strength in politics would have led to more responsive services and policies. This is an aspect of what we may call differential incorporation, whereby some groups are drawn into or penetrate the mainstream arrangements for welfare (or jobs) while others do not. Likewise, strength in the labour market - itself sometimes conferring political muscle - may be mirrored by high status in access to various forms of welfare provision. A second political consideration concerns levels of consumer empowerment, for the degree of consumer control may well vary in relation to the channels by which 'welfare' provisions are secured. Thus, for example, those who receive direct support through a service which stigmatizes them may well have the lowest level of control over the use of the resources. In general terms, the line of argument in chapter 2 seeks to 'theorize' empowerment by placing it in the context of the social division of welfare.

Urban policy limitations and social policy traditions

Chapter 3 considers the impact of urban policies in a context of inequality facing minority ethnic groups. UK direct social policy interventions have offered less than expected to minority ethnic communities, despite rhetoric about assisting inner urban areas. One reason is an overwhelmingly paternalistic and centralizing tradition which has largely ignored pluralism and localism, and has generally built on a conception of need and preference which disregards cultural diversity and racism. 'Special' provision for minorities has been relatively marginal in spending terms, while mainstream provision has been little affected by concern for their needs. Genuine empowerment of groups and communities at local level has not been a strong feature of central government strategies, so that participation has rarely meant a large measure of real power for poor people. Linked with these characteristics is a strong concern for order and control, allied with a tendency to pathologize the poor or disadvantaged as undeserving and responsible for their own circumstances. There has been a long history of stereotyping and stigmatizing 'less deserving' groups, in housing as in other fields, and social order considerations have never seemed far away. Not surprisingly, black people have sometimes been cast amongst the 'less respectable' by public sector agencies. Few of the best potential forms of collective or individual empowerment have been open to them.

A second reason for the limited impact of policies has been the significance of economic liberalism as a determinant of the limits of public action and of the character of policy implementation. (For a neo-Marxist this would need to be understood by being tied into the structural necessities, ideologies and contradictions of many modern welfare states.) Ideas about urban regeneration have often been property-led, since marketeers may see it as more fitting to subsidise capital investment than to prioritize particular categories of household, worker or consumer. Even more fundamental, there is hostility in economic liberalism to localism and so-called 'tribalism', and pressure for competitive bids and markets rather than local political decisions or local collective empowerment. Economic liberalism appears fairly well entrenched in the outlook of the European Community on competition as well as at British government level. (We explore the implications of 'competition' in a specific housing investment field in chapter 6.) As far as concepts of empowerment itself are concerned, economic liberalism tends to prioritize the role of the supposedly sovereign consumer, who chooses in isolation in a market. This sometimes denies people's own definitions of what would empower them, and of the balance preferred between the individual and collective in their lives.

The individual and collective strategies of housing consumers

As we have been implying, people's strategies and actions have to be considered to some extent in the context of the restricting environment of social policy traditions, which constrain redistributional and empowering efforts aimed at helping the disadvantaged. Nonetheless, pressures from communities and groups may emerge for fairer outcomes and meaningful participation, and demands for an increased pluralism within mainstream services. In the housing field individuals and households may pursue a variety of paths to overcome racist obstacles and improve their circumstances, including purchasing owner-occupied dwellings. They may also act together with others in various ways. One collective strategy pursued by excluded groups is to put pressure on mainstream agencies through political action; another is to turn to separatism or particularism, seeking the creation of new agencies or mechanisms to prioritize and serve their interests and needs. This occurred in housing during the 1980s, with the emergence of the black voluntary housing movement, which is discussed in chapter 5. Before that discussion, in the preceding chapter, we set out some of the basic background information on UK housing conditions for black and minority ethnic groups, comment on the research record, and highlight the importance of the strategies pursued by households and larger groupings.

The black voluntary housing movement is looked at particularly in the context of its relationship to a specific programme pursued by the English Housing Corporation from the mid 1980s onwards. We trace the development of this programme up to the early 1990s, and its implications for empowerment and incorporation. It appears more or less unique within British social policy, being an attempt to modify a large mainstream spending programme by giving support for a kind of separatism in organizational development. The Corporation's strategy for black and minority ethnic housing associations sought to help create, build or sustain organizations run primarily by black people, and operating in the interests of minority ethnic communities. The programme was not without its difficulties and tensions, not least the financial pressures of what was an increasingly commercializing environment for housing development by the late 1980s. Nonetheless it stands out as an astonishing achievement for housing activists and Corporation personnel, and is completely out of line with what might have been expected from UK social policy in the Thatcher and Major years. (Indeed, it may not be very easy to find many close or equally significant parallels in other complex industrial societies in North America or Western Europe.) This UK experience raises important questions about the nature of social policy in somewhat fragmented societies, and about the characteristics, limitations and implications of pluralism in the 1990s and beyond. The black voluntary housing movement also demonstrates some differing facets of demands for empowerment, which may have cultural, anti-racist and property dimensions.

Housing investment and production as collective issues

Chapter 6 deals with social housing investment and local community economic development. Since social housing investment could be a potential key factor in inner city regeneration, the indirect socioeconomic impact of housing and other welfare expenditures in urban areas needs to be considered. Seen from the perspective of a local community, this could mean that housing programmes should not be evaluated solely in terms of who gets housed. An evaluation would need to take into account the work created by major building projects, and the impact on local firms and tradespeople. This might apply to other kinds of public investment (roads, hospitals, schools, etc.), yet few effective efforts have been made to monitor impact. Taking findings from housing association case studies, our empirical work supported by the Joseph Rowntree Foundation has demonstrated how small is the economic benefit which passes into minority ethnic communities via contracts awarded to black run firms. The chapter describes the chief research findings here, their implications, and the prospects for targeting some of the investment in ways that would represent better value for money in terms of urban regeneration. This leads briefly into questions about competition, and the way that local empowerment can conflict with economic liberalism. There are options for reshaping social policy approaches, however, which might overcome some of the tensions.

Some conclusions about welfare movements, pluralism, empowerment and the welfare state

In chapter 7, three of the more general or theoretical concerns are brought together. Firstly, it is argued that the politics of 'black housing issues' - while specific - have relevance to understanding new social welfare movements and mobilizations over social policies. A key feature is the interaction with state agencies in a situation where 'the state' is heavily involved with the management of consumption by households. While pressures from the grass roots can help shape public policies, there can also be scope for a degree of incorporation, so that the activities of state agencies may influence the directions and forms of collective social action. Secondly, when it comes to collective empowerment, there are often likely to be externally set limitations on what can be achieved for communities. Just as individual household strategies operate in settings which restrict their success, so group or community efforts also face constraints. The limits lie partly in the precarious nature of assistance founded on principles of selectivity within a complex welfare state, partly in the predispositions of economic liberalism, and partly in the inevitable tensions between centralism and localism as well as between collective and individual decision making. The significance of property rights is also worth noting in relation to empowerment, collective mobilization and individual strategies.

Thirdly, the implications of separatism, particularism and localism are by no means always beneficial for households. Alongside many positive features, the scope for negative discrimination, exclusiveness and abuse of power points towards a case for some kinds of universalism in social policies, despite the attractions of pluralism. Universalism of rights and resource entitlement systems could be seen as an essential defence or protection for the individual in situations where a genuine pluralism emerges. This theme is followed through in our concluding chapter, where some options for the future of social policy in complex urban societies are discussed, bearing in mind the findings of earlier chapters. Governments that wish to manage the demands of ethnic diversity, while restructuring welfare in the direction of participation and choice, may find separatism on the agenda sooner or later; perhaps especially where there is a heavy historical burden of inequality and disadvantage.

Definitions and uses of terms in the book

The word *community* is used throughout this book without specific theoretical connotations. It is primarily treated as a convenient way to refer to groups of people living in particular localities, and can be taken to imply some linkages between households, perhaps based on kinship, mutual obligations, religion, culture, shared services and environment, collective purposes, or common lifestyle. Werbner refers to 'moral communities' being constituted through 'shared suffering', as well as through 'mutual welfare and internal giving to religious or communal causes' (Werbner and Anwar, 1991,p.30). Such a use of the term may well be appropriate for some of the circumstances at issue in this book, but we do not assume a definition of this type. Indeed we accept that the term is a potentially contested one, and can become a convenience for policy makers as much as a reality at the grass roots. It is worth citing Werbner again, for she also notes that state funding can depend on 'fictions' of communal unity, and that funding can divide 'immigrant communities, somewhat arbitrarily, into discrete ethnic groups', and imply that 'each such group is an undivided unity' (p.33). In social policy contexts we need to remember the potentially artificial nature of officially defined communities, but also the prospect that community formation may occur in relation to a specific political and policy environment. Eade refers to the process whereby community has been constructed 'within the wider arena of political representation' (see 1989,pp.2-3,14-15,etc.). Although there may be complex interrelationships here - between community formation, representation, and social movements - these lie outside the scope of our book. For present purposes the word community will be used merely as an identifier of a simple descriptive type, a convenient shorthand only.

The words *black and ethnic minority* also require comment. Physical or biological concepts of 'races' are extremely unreliable and discredited. Even so, the salience of 'race' as a social construct - 'culturally, politically and economically constituted' (Smith, 1989,p.3) - means that we need some reasonably understood identifiers when discussing the differentiated experiences of groups. We can refer to people of migrant origin or descent, who experience discrimination, but racialized minorities need not necessarily have much else in common apart from adverse treatment. Nonetheless the term 'black' is sometimes applied in a broad way in the UK to include a variety of groups (with origins in Africa, the Caribbean, India, China, etc.), all experiencing hostility. This can have value as a politically purposive definition orientated towards

10

solidarity in response to racism. An alternative often found in UK literature, however, is to use the terms Asian or South Asian, Chinese, African/Caribbean, and so forth, or to disaggregate and refer to still more specific groupings. In these circumstances 'black' comes to be defined more narrowly (as in the census analyses referred to in chapter 4). Other terms that appear often in official and academic publications are 'ethnic minorities' and 'minority ethnic groups'. This tends to be a broadly applied terminology, often with a supposed contrast of 'colour' consciously or unconsciously built in; non-white (ethnic minority) as against white. The terminology is certainly contestable, since ethnicity is not - and colour is certainly not - a reliable or watertight concept (see Rattansi, 1994,pp.52-3). On the other hand the use of minority ethnic is very widespread, and is often qualified by linking it with black. Likewise, white and non-white are frequently used words. Today there are also variations in terminology linked to cultural or religious identity; for instance references might be found to Muslims, or Asian Muslims, implying groups with specific origins (although adherence to Islam in reality need not of course have a 'colour' or 'ethnic' implication).

In this book we try to use terms in ways that will make meanings clear, but without intending to imply much about the details of identities or differences. We follow recent official practices to some extent, referring often to minority ethnic, or black minority ethnic, or black and minority ethnic, all with similar purposes. We also use black from time to time, usually with a fairly broad rather than narrow meaning. The choices are often made in order to vary the text rather than to point up a perceived difference. Sometimes other terms related to migrant origins are used where appropriate (as with references to census material), or where they have been used in publications or by people at grass roots. Occasionally the term non-white is used (although this seems rather negative), and quite often the word white. When discussing organizations and firms the book tends to refer to 'black run' or ethnic minority organizations, implying a wide rather than narrow definition, and meaning majority control. In effect, we concentrate on conveying the material and ideas that are our central concerns, while acknowledging that our use of terms is open to challenge.

Notes

1. The writer has begun some comparative work seeking information on minority ethnic housing organizations outside the UK. So far, however, this research has been confined to correspondence with a limited number of scholars and other informants. See Appendix to chapter 5.

2 Social policy, citizenship and empowerment

This chapter provides a perspective on inequalities, power and welfare systems. It begins by discussing the social division of welfare, whereby groups that are already disadvantaged appear to have their inferior status confirmed by exclusion from many of the best benefits of the contemporary welfare state. This is then linked up with the question of citizenship, and processes of incorporation, through which groups or interests may be drawn into the political and welfare forum. In the third part of the chapter some implications are considered by looking at empowerment, entitlement, and stigma. An important aim of this chapter and the next one is to set out analyses which will serve as background to later more detailed material on minority ethnic experiences.

Connections between power and the structure of welfare systems are crucial. We argue that, in the process of obtaining access to welfare, marginalised groups tend to have less opportunities for 'empowerment' than do better placed ones, and that support for the marginalised often carries implications of stigma or social control more strongly than does 'mainstream' welfare provision. We will include comment on meanings of the term empowerment, and will use the case of owner-occupation as a specific illustration. Empowerment is not a word applicable only to specific disadvantaged groups that temporarily become a focus for some governmental programme. Instead *empowerment is a process operating in a differentiated way across and throughout the structures and practices of the welfare state*. Analyses of grass roots strategies and movements need to be informed by an awareness of the ways in which empowerment is structured within welfare systems.

Inequality, the state, and the social division of welfare

We are unlikely to present an effective analysis of the modern welfare state or comment usefully on social welfare movements without first outlining some basic features of the relative disadvantage and deprivation which appear to characterize many aspects of life in an urban society. Central to an understanding of disadvantage is the role played by state institutions and practices. Our concern is not to define or sketch relative poverty and its dimensions, nor to enter the debates over its extent.[1] There is plenty of empirical material available elsewhere to demonstrate that inequalities are not only important, but are patterned in ways that suggest some consistency in who the losers are over time. The patterns now seem so strong and permanent that some observers on right and left have begun talking about an underclass, or class apart, for whom many of the expectations widespread elsewhere do not apply.[2] Given the weight of existing literature on these matters we can safely confine our coverage of the conditions of relative deprivation to a consideration of ethnic minorities and their housing and related concerns (in chapter 4). What is important now, however, is to confront the question of causation, by highlighting some factors in it that are significant for our overall analysis; in particular, we need to address the question of the role of state institutions in relation to patterns of relative disadvantage.

Inequalities in the material conditions of life do not arise simply because people are different from each other, or because of some supposedly fixed features of 'human nature' which lead to selfish competitive behaviour. Nor do patterns of inequality result inevitably from the operation of 'natural laws' of economics, or from the unrestricted and 'efficient' operation of private markets. Undoubtedly, the operation of labour markets and movements of private capital help shape the differences between places, and the variations in people's opportunities and wealth. The decline of a particular industry or the growing significance of certain types of employment practice can have a huge impact on local communities and households. Indeed, so important have some recent changes been that writers have referred to major processes of economic restructuring (see for instance Cooke, 1989, chapter 1, etc.), and to new ways of managing labour power. The disappearance of some traditional forms of manufacturing employment, the increasing dependence on short term or part time working contracts, and the changing balance between men's and women's labour, are all highly significant. Yet many such changes are mediated or encouraged by national governments (within their own nation states and through their interaction in transnational networks where rules or policies are laid down). Even if some governments appear to have less control than they once did over their own national economies, the way they regulate business and social life still has great effects on the distribution of wealth, opportunities and 'life chances'. The pervasiveness and systematic impact of state involvement is rarely acknowledged fully, even in accounts of modern welfare states, and the distribution of costs and benefits through this involvement remains under-researched.

The lack of recognition of the extent of state involvements brings a number of problems. Most important, some political discourse on welfare is influenced by an over-narrow conception of what the state actually does. Somehow we are led into treating state action as concerned primarily with diverting monies from taxation into a range of expenditures that serve 'general need', assist the particularly needy, or involve exercising 'arms length' regulation over economic life to protect basic standards (of environment, behaviour, etc.). 'Interference' and especially redistribution by the welfare state is assumed frequently to concern a transfer of resources from rich to poor. That this perception is an oversimplification can be demonstrated by five examples.

Five examples of the role of the state

Firstly, on the taxation front, it is only surprisingly recently that tax reliefs have come explicitly into the frame of political debate as a form of distributional 'intervention' by governments. Their significance has been long understood by a few perceptive writers (notably since Titmuss, 1958). Yet these more 'hidden' aspects of welfare have often been lost sight of as writers have continued to deploy narrow stereotypes based on direct social services and income maintenance expenditures. This path was followed even in some admired 1970s accounts of the welfare state, written by critical academics journeying up the intellectual cul de sac of crisis theory. The danger was of analyses which undervalued both the significance of fiscal concessions to households or employees, and the links between hidden forms of welfare and intra-class divisions (for instance Gough, 1979). Today we need to recognise that tax concessions are indeed part of the welfare system, and that they benefit very specific groups.[3]

A second example can be found in the images we have of the labour market, which may exaggerate freedom of choice and autonomy. Governments are involved in education and training, and in regulating the world of work. Even the comfortable British notion of an independent tradition of professional skills and commitment cannot be taken entirely at face value (see for example Harrison and Pollitt, 1994,p.3). In earlier days some classic professions were heavily linked with imperial structures of power and with the emergence of state institutions (Johnson, 1982), while recent trends have indicated the capacity of government to downgrade professional activity or autonomy in quest of Conservative Party labour market goals (see for instance Shaw, 1990; Drakeford, 1993). Clearly there are limits on employee autonomy in the defining of work roles and on

14

independence of labour, even for some elite groups; state sponsorship and sanction may be crucial to bargaining power or to the 'transmission of cultural capital' (Savage, Barlow, Dickens and Fielding, 1992,p.28,etc.). This may have many distributional consequences. Certainly at the level of trade union industrial action the stance of government has proved crucial in the UK recently. The extent of workplace rights and the degree to which demands for participation are acknowledged can have enormous impact on distributional outcomes. At a broader level the institutions of the state play a role in middle class formation itself, and in reinforcing or undermining divisions between workers (Savage, Barlow, Dickens and Fielding, 1992).

A third example concerns some assumptions of right wing critics of the welfare state. Economic liberals (or anti-collectivists) tend to favour distribution and resource allocation proceeding via private markets, built around a system of well defined property rights, and with what they would perceive as minimum state 'intervention'. Few right wing anti-collectivist writers, however, seem to have worried much about the fact that without state recognition (and state financed law and order systems in particular) there would be little certainty over rights claims to ownership or inheritance. The way ownership is circumscribed and defined changes over time and is closely linked with sanction by state agencies and laws, which are themselves a product of politics and power (see Harrison, 1987). So the economic liberal's image of a non-interventionist or 'minimal state' may look somewhat disingenuous. There can be few forms of state 'intervention' that have more significant effects on the distribution of wealth than a group of laws which confirms or provides a specific set of property rights and possibilities of inheritance. Indeed we could choose to characterize the UK's system of inheritance, and its low or avoidable taxation on large inherited capital, as a welfare system specifically benefiting the very well to do! Furthermore, there always seem to be new areas where property rights can be conferred on a select group of corporate 'owners'. The exploitation of North Sea oil is a case in point, and there are many people in Scotland who would regard this as equivalent to theft of a national common resource by outsiders. Do right wing theorists really wish to suggest that the taxation of private profits gained from the licensed exploitation of natural resources is an 'interference' with free markets? Equally sustainable would be the view that the use of such revenues by the state to prop up various forms of welfare for poorer people could be interpreted as an income for recipients derived from their just claims to a share in these property resources.

Sadly, the concept of a right to a 'dividend' from a share in natural resources figures little in rhetoric about citizenship. Anti-collectivists would be threatened by such a concept, while academic theorists of the left remain uninterested in property issues, and ignorant of their significance. The consequence is that we are led to assume that the poor in particular receive benefits through the generosity of the 'owners' of private property, who are public spirited enough to pay up with only an occasional outburst.

Fourthly, and connected intimately with property rights, is the framework for corporate activity established through state laws, regulation, etc. In the UK and elsewhere in the west it is almost taken for granted that companies can have 'rights' analogous to (or even greater than) those acknowledged for individual people, yet there is no particular ethical justification for this that could not be fiercely contested. The granting to companies of powers of compulsory purchase or powers to restrain individual liberty (as with a private prison or security activity) might be viewed as conferring quite unacceptable power upon private sector profit makers. At a more structural level, laws or state practices encouraging the growth of large investment funds may have helped reshape capital itself. The UK's occupational pension funds, insurance companies and building societies have grown at least partly as elements in the structure of the welfare state, so that 'welfare' has actually led to a reconstruction of 'private' capital (see Harrison, 1984,p.37).

Fifthly, governments have frequently invested in industries and in infrastructure in ways that have influenced the relative chances for people in different localities, the profitability of particular companies, and the relative prosperity of one group as against another. The 'defence' industries, or the encouragement of private road transport, are complex examples of this. For the latter, it seems reasonable to suggest that the losers from road building programmes might include the huge numbers of children affected by asthma (if the link between the illness and motor traffic pollution turns out to be strong), the households affected by noise and disturbance (especially in inner urban areas), and those hit hard by the decline of public transport. No genius is required to see that the chief beneficiaries are the middle class able bodied white males among whom car ownership or use is high, especially if they can commute to pleasant localities away from the polluted inner cities. It is not necessarily straightforward to work out any kind of detailed balance sheet of costs and benefits arising as a result of public sector investments, and such an exercise is often fruitless. Attempts to determine the beneficiaries of some infrastructure programmes or general services are useful, however (see Le Grand, 1982; Bramley, Le Grand and Low, 1989), and more research would be welcome.

What is important for present purposes - in this example as in the other four - is to recognise that there is widespread involvement of governments, law and state agencies in daily life, and that this has a great variety of distributional and redistributional consequences. Put differently, the welfare state is not just a mechanism that intervenes in, and possibly 'corrects', the structure of inequality; it is 'in its own right' a system of stratification and 'an active force in the ordering of social relations' (Esping-Andersen, 1990,p.23). It is indeed an active force in the ordering and re-ordering of capital itself.

Political factors and forces

None of what has been argued so far should be taken to imply the presence of an all powerful state, capable of dominating both capital and labour. No state is likely to be satisfactorily depicted as a unified entity, acting as if it had a purpose, nor are governments likely to be able to act very independently of their state's particular economic environment. Rather, state activities and the welfare state itself have grown as politics and administration have become concerned with the management and organizing of processes of consumption, distribution and production, and with the regulation of daily life. State agencies may respond to a variety of pressures, of which those from industrial and financial capital are often most significant (for relevant material see Crouch and Dore, 1990; Harrison, 1984; Ingham, 1984). Room to manoeuvre may be circumscribed sharply by the power of economic interests; in the UK the City of London has operated as a crucial restraint on industrial performance (and perhaps indirectly on the capacity for corporatist relationships in industrial development). Yet even so there has been scope for a wide array of influences operating through political channels (including organized labour). Patterned inequalities may ultimately derive from the characteristics of capitalistic economic relationships and structures, from longstanding cultural or religious attitudes (such as attitudes to disability; see Barnes forthcoming), and from patriarchal traditions; but the institutions of the state may have some independent effects in mediating and regulating in the labour market, in the control of property, and in the consumption sphere. Variations between welfare states may reflect the histories of political class coalitions (Esping-Andersen, 1990,p.1), grass roots disturbances, pressures from religious institutions, the impact of wars, imperial and colonial histories, and a variety of other conditions. Esping-Andersen employs the term 'welfare-state regimes', to denote that 'in the relation between state and economy a complex of legal and organizational features are systematically interwoven' (p.2). It is important, however, not to try too hard to find regularities or straightforward bases for classification when comparing countries, since they may have very different histories and cultures. Consequently the idea of regimes of welfare needs to be approached cautiously, and we certainly cannot assume that such regimes will be the same in different parts of the world, or that the meanings and distributional impacts of public policies will be similar. The political and economic forces shaping welfare outcomes in different settings are likely to be very varied. Even so, there may be some common features, not least the ability of politically well placed groups and

17

interests to secure a firm place in governmental welfare arrangements. The position of black minority ethnic groups in relation to welfare systems may be one of disadvantage in many countries.

Consumption and the social division of welfare

If we focus on the consumption field in particular, then the idea of the social division of welfare is helpful in addressing the question of distributional patterns (Titmuss, 1958; Sinfield, 1978; Harrison, 1986; Mann, 1992). This falls in the realms of 'middle range' theory. The basic idea is that there are several channels or systems through which households or consumers receive welfare. The channels include fiscal routes (via tax concessions related to some aspect of consumption such as owner-occupied housing), occupational routes (related to jobs, such as company cars or pension schemes), and public or social welfare (the more direct provisions through state directed services and administered financial payments). Forms of welfare from the different systems may overlap, as in the case of company cars (which are simultaneously a fiscal and occupational benefit), but in all instances there is likely to be state sanction or involvement. No simple boundary can be drawn between these systems and the monies earned or acquired through employment, especially since taxation concessions impinge on the effective value or usefulness of most salaries and private investments; indeed the social division of welfare thesis recognises this more satisfactorily than do cruder models of welfare systems. On the other hand, the elements identified in the thesis do constitute a reasonable preliminary model for analysing the ensemble of state activities in the welfare sphere that supplements or enhances direct wages.

The initial formulation of the social division of welfare thesis by Titmuss has subsequently been criticized and supplemented substantially, and we need to be aware that there are issues that the Titmuss framework did not tackle adequately, notably the relationships between gender and welfare (but see Rose, 1981), and the question of infrastructure investments. Apart from being bought directly at full price from wages, or offered through the channels highlighted by Titmuss, welfare is also provided or supported via general infrastructure spending and through legal arrangements over property, as we indicated earlier in this chapter. It is also supplied by individuals - usually women - on an unpaid basis in the home, and by men and women on a voluntary basis in the wider community in a variety of settings. In both these contexts state institutions may have a significant influence on how activity is organized, who the beneficiaries are, and who carries the costs. Unwaged domestic labour clearly forms an important part of the welfare state. Again it is difficult to make any simple separation of this labour from the world of paid work and purchased welfare. For example, some middle class households find it possible to substitute extensive directly purchased welfare services (and house and garden maintenance services) for domestic labour by the household's members. Gregson and Lowe (1994) offer a fascinating study of some aspects of this, covering employment of cleaners, nannies, etc. Clearly the area of domestic labour is an aspect of the welfare state which has changed considerably since Titmuss wrote his key paper. Nonetheless, despite the limitations and omissions of analysis, the basic thesis of the social division of welfare has stood the test of time very well.

One striking feature of arrangements in the UK is the way in which status in welfare terms seems to connect with other markers of social position and division. Those who are dependent primarily on the direct public or social channels of welfare may be differentiated from others who are far less dependent on direct assistance, but derive more from fiscal or occupational welfare. People who have a weak position in relation to the labour market will be least likely to benefit from fiscal or occupational welfare. Although social policies may themselves come to influence the development of relative life chances and stratification, fragmentation in welfare systems does seem to link with wider inequalities rooted in economic activity and socioeconomic power. As Sinfield puts it, the 'very concept of a social division of welfare underlines the link with the stratification system of a society' and 'the need to relate analyses of the two' (1978, p.131). Where a public/social service is offered on a genuinely universal basis - more or less still the case with the British National Health Service - questions of stigma and differentiation are less likely to arise (although they may occur), so the debate over universalism and selectivity is relevant here.

Differential incorporation and citizenship

A discussion of the social division of welfare can lead into some questions about the meanings of citizenship, and the politics of representation in social policy. It should be clear from comments so far that we perceive the welfare state as heavily implicated in the management and organization of consumption by households, across a wide range of activities (housing, leisure, environment, pensions, transport, etc.). Mention has also been made of the ability of politically well placed groups to secure a firm place in government sponsored welfare arrangements. We now need to look further both at differentiation and politics.

In earlier work the present writer suggested that households have access to 'consumption bundles' in which the state is involved through the operation of the social division of welfare (Harrison, 1986). This is linked to a process of differential incorporation - material and political - through which wealthier people gain greatly. They are drawn in, acknowledged, and represented.

19

politically, and their consumption, inheritances and life styles are underpinned by state institutions. Some parts of the package on offer are so beneficial that they encourage not merely the supply of immediate needs, but also the accumulation of capital by the household or the development of subsequent earnings capacity. Less well off people are unlikely to experience the same advantages. The variations in access to state sponsored welfare for different groups may be systematic, and linked with other attributes of the household in terms of labour market status and opportunities, gender, disability, ethnicity, possibilities for inherited wealth, etc. The operation of the social division of welfare may contribute to intergenerational effects, and to what amounts to a cycle of transmitted advantage.

Here we are turning an underlying theme of the underclass debate on its head (as it deserves). For it is not only the transmission of deprivation from generation to generation that requires study, but also the transmission of control over wealth, opportunity and power. In constructing a useful theory about social divisions or social action it would be mistaken to start with the deprived and their behaviour, since it is plausible that the key to understanding their situation lies in relating it to that of better placed groups (and the mechanisms whereby the position of those groups is maintained). Indeed it is not impossible that self definitions (and perhaps political or cultural consciousness) amongst marginalised people are influenced heavily by the pattern and character of exclusion itself. On the one hand is the prospect of demoralization which can follow from rejection or stigmatization, with the option that people will withdraw into more private worlds. On the other hand - and more important - is the possibility that those who are excluded and stigmatized may create alternatives to the mainstream in areas which are within their control. Perhaps a group may emphasize particular forms of dress or language, construct or reaffirm strong musical or arts traditions, or develop independent solidarities, political voices and mobilizations. From this perspective perhaps even ethnicity could be argued to be partly a manifestation of the politics of exclusion and representation. While some minority ethnic groups may choose to assert the need for making common cause under the banner of black identity, others may turn to religion or culture connected with the origins or roots of their communities. In both cases there can be a strong element of resistance to the dominant cultures and interests of 'white society'. While it would be wrong to overgeneralize, at the very least there are likely to be links between the politics of identity and the politics of exclusion. Thus processes of differential incorporation may influence and be influenced by the politics of identity.

What we have been doing in discussing implications of differential incorporation is, in a sense, looking at patterns of citizenship. Citizenship is very much about relationships between individuals, groups, rights, duties and state institutions; it is also about relative degrees of incorporation and empowerment. Perhaps the experience and construction of citizenship is multi-faceted, with people's roles and status in the context of work, national boundaries, legal systems, politics, or voluntary and cultural organizations, all having importance for them. In any event, amongst its possible attributes effective citizenship certainly means being included in the systems of rights and welfare provisions that are mediated or managed by state agencies, and having one's needs met through mainstream political intermediation. Thus the persons who enjoy the fullest measure of citizenship in the UK are likely to have access to a range of channels which provide security and welfare, and to receive benefits without a loss of status or being subjected to some kind of 'therapy'. Their needs are probably acknowledged through effective political channels. If citizenship is partly about inclusion of these kinds, then we are looking at situations where citizenship is itself experienced *very* differently by differing groups, and shifts over time for them.[4] Some groups are drawn into the mainstream of political representation, receive relatively good support from the state's institutions, and appear to be part of the 'welfare state deal'. If the welfare state is an ensemble of modes of representation (or intermediation) and regulation, some people benefit very strongly from it. Others are on the fringes of the welfare state, marginalised politically, sometimes receiving stigmatized services, and from time to time battling to enter mainstream political channels (for further discussion see chapter 4; also cf Oliver and Zarb, 1989).

There is no reason to assume a beneficial 'evolutionary' process whereby the rights and status of citizenship grow over the years. We can envisage situations where factors such as widespread unemployment for young people, the destruction of reputable or meaningful training and recruitment routes for skilled workers, or the downgrading of schools in poor areas through lack of resources, might be linked to processes of 'de-incorporation' for sections of youth. This might actually erode the basis of citizenship, insofar as that is linked with political obligations and rights based on participation, identity, or a sense of legitimacy about the worlds of work and education.

Looking at the overall pattern, and borrowing terminology from Lustiger-Thaler and Shragge (1993), we can refer to 'the differential distribution of ...rights of inclusion' (p.163), and a conscious 'politics of recognition' (p.162). The politics of recognition and citizenship include struggles by disadvantaged groups to enter the political and welfare mainstream or establish viable alternatives, but such battles do not necessarily take place on ground chosen by the outsider groups. Analysis of the politics of representation in the field of consumption is anyway likely to be fairly complex, since it ought to acknowledge not only visible actions and movements but also less visible networks, allegiances and constituencies. The idea of differential incorporation is useful in that context, capturing as it does the sense of a range of levels and extents to which groups are accommodated and integrated in the welfare state, consciously or unconsciously. 'Rights' of inclusion may be tightly tied to positional factors such as relationships to mainstream political parties and constituencies, labour market status, etc. In times of rapid changes in socioeconomic structure, and when more pluralism is being discussed amongst politicians and practitioners, many new demands for fuller inclusion may come onto the agenda of public politics, and conscious collective actions may be evident. It will be an open question as to how far any particular welfare state will accommodate emergent forces and demands. Chapter 5 is partly about one such set of demands, and the prospects of 'new' groups achieving a measure of incorporation.

Empowerment, entitlement and stigma

Having sketched out an overview of the character of the welfare state, the social division of welfare, and differential incorporation, we now seek to place the concept of empowerment in relation to the structures we have been describing. Earlier sections have noted the divisive character of welfare institutions and practices, and how this connects with differential experiences of citizenship. Empowerment can be treated as a facet of citizenship, and (similarly) is experienced differently by different groups of people. We will suggest below that it is best analysed by being considered in relation to better off groups as well as poorer ones, and by being linked to the social division of welfare. Owner-occupation provides examples of potentially empowering forms of state support, while residualized and stigmatized services can illustrate disempowerment. In determining outcomes the state plays crucial roles for both. Prospects for empowerment connect with broad patterns of advantage and disadvantage.

Defining empowerment and participation

There is a developing literature on empowerment, with contributions from a range of perspectives (for a stimulating example see Baistow, 1994/95). In fact the term is not easy to define in any precise way without specifying contexts. In fields such as housing, or urban renewal, empowerment clearly means more than the word participation. It has long been recognised that participation itself is a variable concept, and can involve degrees or levels ranging from mere tokenism on the part of a decision taking agency to genuine sharing of power with consumers (see for instance Arnstein, 1969; cf JRF, 1994g). Much the same is true of official involvements with empowerment. Public agencies may simply consult their clients, or may go further and include them in decision making committees, or may hand over power to them in a variety of ways.[5] A public policy of empowering a community might mean giving them powers that they did not previously possess, but still fall short of passing over certain powers held by public agencies. Apart from this gradation in the degree of control passed over, there is variation in the scope of that control. Taking housing as an example, empowerment might mean consumers - collectively or individually - having rights over design, construction, alteration, daily use, occupation, or sale. Indeed empowerment might mean being able to choose whether to have subsidy in an individual or collectively managed form; whether households wished to act collectively or as individuals. It might mean control over the investment and capital itself, for instance permitting a community or group to determine how and to whom a contract for building or upgrading houses was awarded. This control of the capital or investment could cast empowerment in a very different light from simply providing a state subsidy governed by the giver. This is an issue touched on later in chapter 7.

One danger in considering empowerment would be to place it solely in relation to the poor and previously disempowered. That is how the term is sometimes used, being taken to express a change brought about for specific groups as a result of new resources or methods of managing a service or development. At its worst, 'empowering people' is then in danger of becoming primarily part of a professional practice repertoire of therapeutic strategies. Using the term in this narrow way to apply to the disadvantaged could have major weaknesses. It would make comparative evaluation of forms of empowerment difficult, and would diverge from the type of welfare state analysis argued for above. We need to be able to compare what is done for the poor with what is done for the better off to understand empowerment as an aspect of welfare state processes and politics. This means trying to locate empowerment in relation to the operation of the social division of welfare. To do that fully here would take too much space, but we can indicate some possible lines of argument in an outline way. We will start with an example. If the management of consumption is a field where a degree of empowerment can be achieved for consumers in line with their status and place in the systems of welfare provision, then owner-occupation can provide a 'case study' of this process in operation in the UK.

Owner-occupation as one basis for empowerment?

It might be argued that the 'highest' form of empowerment in the early 1980s in UK housing would appear to have involved the following: to be receiving a large amount of tax relief to help buy one's house, to be given assistance with costs if a move in one's job meant moving house, to be assured of security of possession

23

and of the capital gains (free of taxation), to have the right to sell or transmit the property, to be able to borrow against it, and to have a good chance of protection from dramatic physical disturbance through planning and building control (while retaining the right to make modest changes to one's own dwelling). At the same time the truly empowered occupant would be in an attractive area where state and private provision of services was excellent, with low insurance premiums and good prospects of capital value appreciation, with ample and secure parking space adjacent to the dwelling, and where dangers of burglary and other intrusions would be relatively low.

To achieve the above benefits the household would usually need access to a secure income, and the full range of circumstances we have outlined would not apply for every owner. Owner-occupation is not a unified experience for all home owners, nor is it free of difficulties (Forrest and Murie, 1994; JRF, 1992c,1993c,1994f; Karn, Kemeny and Williams, 1985). Indeed, ownership itself is not a fixed set of rights and duties unvarying over time and place. Even so, some scholars have certainly argued that it has had special merits and attractions for the consumer by contrast with renting from public sector landlords (Saunders, 1990). When enjoyed in conjunction with high and secure earnings, the tenure can be very empowering. Key features are that there are *notions of entitlements that have acquired immunity from requiring approval on a daily basis from governmental agents, and that have taken on the appearance of matters of private right rather than public politics.*

The daily use of the house itself in a variety of ways is likely to be less restricted than in some forms of renting, although owner-occupation too may be subject to constraints (such as limitations imposed through covenants or by mortgage lending organizations). As well as influencing enjoyment of leisure and domestic life, this liberty connects back to the world of paid employment too. It is possible that today's residential areas are viewed in a less restrictive way by local planning authorities than once might have been the case, and the rise of certain types of homeworking is not usually subject to restraint because of any very tight conceptions of zoning and segregation of land uses. Consequently the freedoms of ownership can actually enhance relative opportunities in the world of paid employment, since it may be easier to establish or run a business from home than it would be under some tenancy agreements. The tenant may be disadvantaged thereby. For instance, one housing association officer, in a recent review of an edited collection by Gilroy and Woods (1994), observes that her association's tenancy agreements 'expressly forbid' tenants from 'carrying out any form of "business" in their homes'. Such rules might bear harshly on women in particular, if a higher proportion of them need to work from home (see Llewelyn-Davies, 1995). This might also work against people in some minority ethnic communities. The situation may be part of a larger pattern of disadvantage faced by women in the context of a growing owner-occupation sector, since they may often find it more difficult to become owner-occupiers, may become dependent on men for housing consumption, and may share less well in the accumulation of wealth in this sphere (for relevant comments see Little, 1994,pp.156-160; Gilroy and Woods, 1994).

The combination of physical and capital assets for the successful owner-occupier can be impressive. At the upper end of the owner-occupied housing price range there is likely to be plenty of space within homes for work as well as relaxation. Meanwhile the house may become a security for borrowing money for business or consumption purposes on favourable terms. Wealthy owner-occupiers also have some likelihood of being able to inherit housing property from the previous generation, and will be able to assist their own children with housing costs in due course.

The central role of the state in the empowerment and disempowerment of consumers

Our example of owner-occupation illustrates that an individual or household group can benefit and be empowered (or disempowered) in a variety of ways; but it is important to assert once again how central is the role of state institutions here. Empowerment is tied in with the social division of welfare and with the operation and structuring of institutions. The advantages of owner-occupation (and more generally the casting of consumer rights and charters in individualized terms during the 1980s and 1990s), raise questions about mediation and what is often called decommodification. State institutions can mediate between producer or financier on the one hand, and consumer on the other. This is normal practice where professionals supply a service which is subject to uncertain relationships between supplier and client (as in medicine where the client has difficulty in diagnosing her or his needs). Indeed we can see certain professional organizational structures and practices as part of the apparatus of the state, since legal or administrative sanction may be given by governments. In some areas the mediation and sanction may press in the direction of therapy and control for clients as well as care. Thus the offer of a service or support is linked with social control, or the implicit possibility of rejection. Carlen (1994) notes, for instance, how homeless young people can be subjected to processes which deter, deny and discipline. Practitioners in some fields can be cast in the role of policing access to a service, rationing it, and judging the consumer. This may mean that a role of street level bureaucrat (Lipsky, 1980), social gatekeeper or urban manager takes on strong elements of policing or therapy. Perhaps this will apply most often or most oppressively where clients start from a weak position, in financial terms or through deviating from official norms of behaviour or capacity. For them

25

the welfare state may sometimes become the 'therapeutic state' (cf Bean, 1983,p.279).

Outside the areas of 'professional practice' related to care or judging of individuals, however, state sanction or mediation may be a simpler matter, concerned to regulate in the interests of safety, secure favourable terms for consumers, or protect some moral or religious values (as in laws restricting usury in some countries). In our owner-occupation example above, it has apparently been about favourable financial terms, fairer and more honest behaviour by exchange professionals, stability in the market, and - in the 1980s - widening choice and activities in funding through a degree of diversification or deregulation (see for instance Chancellor of the Exchequer, 1984).

Two points need making. First, it may be wrong to think too straightforwardly of 'welfare rights' as being dependent on the extent of decommodification and detachment from economic markets that can be achieved as a result of pressure from the labour movement and other sources. Rights and empowerment might be developed in regulated and stabilized 'private' market situations as well as via direct state services. (For customers, access to private property rights and the opportunity to challenge the producer of a service may be involved.) Inclusion of these possibilities in any account of welfare rights follows logically from the social division of welfare thesis. Second, it may be that consumers who are assisted in this way are more likely to be genuinely empowered by the state than when they are served through non market or non ownership routes. This is an open question, and it can be argued in reply that the individualized citizenship rights of market consumerism are sometimes best protected, supplemented or asserted through collective (political) channels. On the other hand it does seem that legitimacy is harder to challenge in modern western societies when 'private' property rights are involved, and when people are spending some of 'their own money' to buy a service. Other forms of provision (less 'commodified') that are very valuable to people can operate with a high degree of public support over long periods of time, but probably only under certain conditions; with the UK National Health Service, for instance, the near universal availability and wide use of the service, and the heavy involvement of middle class professionals as providers. If we look at non market (and non property) forms of welfare provision that have a more residual character, we may find that mediation sometimes leads to an extremely low level of consumer power, and considerable uncertainties about long term continuity of levels of support.

What we are indicating is that the welfare state has the capacity to assist consumers in many ways, and that some avenues confer or permit a great deal of control of resources by clients, and continuity and certainty over time. Empowerment in welfare cannot be analysed only in terms of conscious efforts to help or respond to defined groups with visible needs or deprivations. It must also be looked at in terms of individuals and less visible collective interests (or constituencies) to which governments may respond, often indirectly rather than by explicit intervention. Well off owner-occupiers may provide an example of such a constituency.

Recent trends; continuity as well as change

In a period when the collective has been de-emphasized in favour of individualism in consumer politics, we could expect enhancement of those forms of empowerment which give prosperous households access to services or assets on an individual basis. Assets may include entitlements to swift (private) medical treatment, private pensions, private (or company) cars, elite state or private schools for children, owner-occupied dwellings, and so forth. Catering for growth in some of these areas may have been easier in periods of buoyancy than at times of severe economic difficulty. The first half of the 1980s may have been far more optimistic for owner-occupation, for example, than was the end of the decade. In the 1990s some kinds of individualized consumption may have become less accessible to households, or available on worse terms. The mortgages market, for instance, probably distinguishes more sharply now between higher and lower risk customers than it did a decade ago. There have also been tensions in the period since 1979 between the desire to respond to consumers and the wish to adopt free market models, accommodate corporate business interests or other producer interests (which may exploit consumers), or carve out new territory for profit making. For example, tax relief for owner-occupiers has lost favour with the Conservatives recently, as it 'distorts' housing markets, reducing the relative viability of private landlordism. Nonetheless, in general terms, state institutions have continued to give sanction or support to middle class consumers (and to many 'respectable' working class ones), in ways which permit or confer a great deal of power or security. Property rights - usually more or less ignored in social policy texts - are deeply involved in this, and played a crucial role in the 1980s. (An example was the extension of ownership through widespread sale of council houses, on a highly discounted basis, to large numbers of the better off among council house tenants.) Political explanations might be found in terms of constituency building by governments, processes of mass level incorporation (whereby groups like the white male skilled working class may be assisted and drawn into the mainstream of welfare and politics), or the advance of democratic notions and rights in general.[6]

At the other end of the social policy 'empowerment scale' we find residual services and provisions which - despite increasing official references to the need for consultation or participation - still confer upon the poor very little chance of control of assets or of planning over time (for relevant comments on time see

Sinfield, 1978, pp.149-50). Residualization of some direct public services has become more marked in the UK during the period since 1979. Dealing with minorities rather than offering a universalistic service, residualized provisions can often do little more than provide a safety net, and are subject to the politics of social pathology. This contrasts sharply with the notion of a politics of mutual sympathy and common security which some collectivists feel might help sustain services that were used by all. Indeed it is in residualized services, or within those rationed amongst working class households, that stigma and labelling can bite on the would-be client or recipient. Households may be 'graded' and classified, practitioners may face dilemmas over giving support or exerting control, and notions of respectability and deviance can come into play to determine treatment or the quality of service available. These are certainly not new phenomena arising in the 1980s. For instance, this kind of situation has been observed frequently for council housing in the past (see for example Tucker, 1966; Damer, 1974), and racism has been shown to play a significant role alongside notions of respectability (for sources see chapter 4). In the era of Conservative Party rule since 1979, however, the theme of the deserving and less deserving may have been re-emphasized or re-interpreted, as directly provided services have been targeted for reconstruction, restriction or reduction.

We have been indicating that in managing the disadvantaged, governments and agencies may be influenced by ideas that cast particular groups as deviant, undeserving, or simply lacking in intelligence. It has also been suggested above that these perceptions are by no means new. It may be worth giving a few examples of the kinds of thinking involved, which conjure up images of control contrasting strongly with the liberties of higher income owner-occupiers to which we referred earlier. Ward (1974) quotes a 1950s council tenant handbook which neatly catches the flavour of a longstanding housing management paternalism. It observes that homes should be kept 'clean and tidy'. Tenants should endeavour to have some method of cleaning as they go along, and 'not try to clean the whole house in one day'. Regular bed times for children and adults are recommended, except on special occasions. Families should 'sit down properly at the table' (p.12). This absurd paternalism may seem mild by comparison with some of the more censorious types of labelling. Tucker's early account of how 'problem families' were perceived shows a highly judgemental consciousness on the part of some officials. Amongst observations he notes are comments on families 'in whose case there is social defectiveness to such a degree that they require supervision and control for their own well-being and that of others' (1966,p.93). Often - in the eyes of an official - a problem family could be a large one, 'some of the children being dull or feeble minded'. From their appearance they may be 'strangers to soap and water, toothbrush and comb' (p.94).

Tucker collected other revealing remarks which still make interesting reading, but attitudes have changed somewhat since 1966. Nonetheless, in a pervasive way there is a degree of continuity here in the UK welfare state. A powerful strand of social pathology thought persists, alongside a genuine concern for household needs. Moves and statements by government ministers in the 1980s and more recently have provided illustrations of the persistence of very hostile judgemental outlooks on specific lifestyles (for instance see Carlen, 1994,pp.33-4). Not surprisingly, therefore, social order considerations impinge upon the vision of policy makers, and some provisions carry an element of discipline and control. The prospects and reception facing some 'latecomers' or new arrivals in the welfare state queue may be even worse than for longstanding clients, especially where racism plays a part.

Of course, official attitudes to poor people are not necessarily always hostile, and there is frequently concern for those held to be deserving. Today there is often an expectation that clients will be consulted about their needs, and attempts have been made to encourage community involvement in certain council housing estate contexts and elsewhere. There has been a change in social policy, with more reference to 'users' and their rights (although this sits uneasily alongside some of government's other goals). The word empowerment has itself come into the official vocabulary from time to time. On the other hand, talk of consultation or participation has to be measured against the extent to which a service is operating in terms of safety nets and therapy rather than entitlements, choices or *meaningful* rights over substantial resources. Furthermore, many residualized forms of support cannot go beyond short term amelioration. *The difficulties of inserting any real concept or practice of empowerment into such situations are immense*, especially if government sets its face against redistributive policies or an increase of financial resources (cf Malpass, 1993).

British government ministers may see community empowerment and certain kinds of tenant rights as a way of mobilizing local forces against social as well as physical decay in social rented housing areas. Yet it is not pathological characteristics that provide the best guides to underlying causation, but the processes of differentiation and exclusion that the welfare state and uneven access to wealth embody. Consequently, struggles for empowerment in UK council estates may look different when seen from grass roots perspectives than from an official view. Ministers may wish to encourage changed behaviour and greater collective responsibility, and may (partly in this cause) even go some way to conferring rights 'to manage', as government has recently done in the context of council housing (see Department of the Environment and Welsh Office, 1994). Members of local communities, by contrast, might want a more favourable rents or housing benefits regime, speedier and better quality repairs and improvements, higher housing and environmental standards, a chance of a transfer to a better estate or new house somewhere else, some opportunities for paid local work on the estate, and more resources in general. This is not to deny that local people will be concerned about combating crime, or about day to day management issues. Rather we are suggesting that there can be underlying factors of poverty, lack of property, and little availability of resources which limit the value of the kinds of empowerment that might be envisaged by some governmental agencies. These factors may mean that certain households are dependent on some very disempowering forms of state treatment in the areas of income maintenance, law and order, or social care. Thus, even while officials are talking about participation on an estate, other official and private sector agents may be subjecting some of its residents to rationing, humiliation or deterrence in another sphere of welfare or services. Put more mildly, the operation of residualized systems is unlikely to give poor people enough long term security and planning capacity to feel genuinely empowered, whatever is being said about them participating. At the same time there may be difficulties in reconciling some of the government's ideas about markets (and compulsory competitive tendering for repairs and services) with local tenant empowerment or equal opportunities concerns (see Fraser, 1993, for the latter).

Conclusions

To conclude this chapter we can summarize by saying that experiences and prospects of empowerment must be seen in the context of the kinds of patterned disadvantage that seem to characterize differentiation and stratification in the welfare state. Some local groups or communities that are excluded from the better opportunities of mainstream welfare will mobilize around issues of need, but certain of their objectives are likely to be difficult to achieve. Limits exist, and these are rooted in the general character of the distribution of resources, power and opportunity. In the next chapter we will look specifically at urban policy, to explore how far it has assisted communities that have otherwise been disadvantaged within the UK welfare state. We shall indicate that the impact of policy appears to have been disappointing, and this raises questions about the limits of grass roots action and the constraints of social policy itself. We will try to highlight those key features of the UK welfare state tradition that have inhibited the effectiveness of urban policy responses to demands for empowerment, greater pluralism, and more resources for the marginalised.

Notes

1. Poverty and deprivation have been defined in varied ways in UK literature. Wide definitions are sometimes used in order to include a range of aspects of disadvantage (although this is not necessarily acceptable to all sides in politics). For instance, Vaux and Divine refer not only to 'financial poverty' but also to the poverty 'that arises from denial of access to other public services such as housing, health care, transport, personal social services etc.' Consequently they see financial poverty as representing 'only one portion' of deprivation (Vaux and Divine, 1988,p.209). When taking a broad view it is important to appreciate that certain experiences of deprivation are easier to measure than are others. Some aspects of a lack of opportunities can be demonstrated readily, while others cannot. For the present study, relative deprivation and disadvantage are assumed to have wide dimensions, ideally needing to be placed in relation to issues like racism, violence against women, or the hostility experienced by disabled people, as well as in more measurable material circumstances. Some features of denial of opportunities have been measured (for instance see JRF, 1991a), but even good statistics may not capture the full depth of a household experience where a large number of limitations and disadvantages reinforce each other on a daily basis.

2. The debate on underclasses is a complex one; for insights see Macnicol, 1987; Mann, 1992; Bagguley and Mann, 1992.

3. A good idea of the importance of tax allowances and reliefs in the 1980s can be gained from Wilkinson, 1993. She refers to an 'explosion in reliefs' (p.211), noting (amongst other developments) that, by the end of the 1980s, encouraging people to save for their pensions cost the government in lost taxes an annual sum equal to one third of the cost of state retirement pensions for existing pensioners.

4. For discussion of gender and citizenship see Lister, 1991 and 1993.

5. There is an extensive literature on participation in housing, with significant studies reported recently; see for instance JRF, 1990,1991,1994g; Clapham, 1993. Self help and self build have been covered to some extent; for instance see National Federation of Housing Associations (NFHA), 1988; JRF, 1990a; Williams and Lusk, 1993. A great deal has also been published on participation in other related policy areas; very recent examples are a Rowntree report on community involvement in City Challenge (JRF, 1994b), and a paper by McArthur (1995) on involvement in strategic community partnerships. Given our limitations of space, this book cannot do justice to the participation literature or research, but it is worth noting that it would be useful to have more material on minority ethnic participation in housing. The

NFHA report (noted above) covers the Zenzele self build scheme which involved mainly unemployed young black people, while Williams and Lusk include minority ethnic organisations.

6. To continue with our specific example, owner-occupation need not be interpreted necessarily as a force for conservatism. At certain times and in some circumstances the growth of home ownership can be interpreted as part of a process of democratization or the extension of rights. There is a role here for pressure from the grass roots as well as an accommodation by state institutions. For North America, Doucet and Weaver provide a fascinating scholarly account relevant to this issue (see 1991,pp.169, 184,421-2,etc.).

3 Urban policies and empowerment: An inevitable failure?

No wide ranging study of 'race', social policy, or housing can avoid mentioning recent urban histories and the policies governments apply to the cities. An analysis of empowerment issues also needs to take account of the urban policy record, because part of the background to the housing strategies that individuals and groups can pursue is the framework of opportunities offered by urban policies. *We need to consider how far patterns of disadvantage and exclusion* mentioned in chapter 2 *may have been modified through explicit governmental 'urban' strategies, and we must review the scope there has been for local community involvement.* We also need to see how much attention has been paid to *facilitating pluralism*, in the sense of accommodating collective locality-based interests that may diverge from the white mainstream. Chapter 2 has already commented briefly on the appearance of ideas about participation and empowerment in recent official discourses, with reference to housing. This needs to be seen in context as one element within a complex history of central and local government approaches.

This chapter will consider governmental responses to urban conditions and inequalities, and the impact of these policies.[1] We will comment on the characteristics of official urban programmes, and on any potential for previously excluded groups to mobilize around services and resources provided through governmental agencies. The chapter will also highlight some *broad characteristics of the UK welfare state which have made it unresponsive to demands for grass roots empowerment and ethnic pluralism*, despite a certain amount of rhetoric about participation. Our critique connects back to chapter 2, for the implication is that inner city policies and their limitations need to be understood in the context of a broader analysis. This should include an overview of the welfare state as a structure that contributes to and manages social differentiation, and that contains and regularizes many features that inhibit options for poorer people and minorities. Chapter 4 will then turn specifically to the experiences of black people, and to the housing research record.

The first section below begins with a reminder that there is a spatial division of welfare, whereby stratification manifests itself in geographical patterns of relative advantage and disadvantage. To this may be added the complexities of a degree of 'racial' segregation. To some extent urban policies have been founded in a recognition of socioeconomic patterns in which inner cities are perceived to have been losing ground for several decades. In addition the situation of minority ethnic groups has been tied in with perceptions of the inner areas. In these contexts a variety of explicitly 'urban' policies have emerged over the post war period. Although 'race' relations have often been on the political agenda here, there is surprisingly little evidence of policies having been targeted or shaped with specific minority ethnic groups in mind. More generally, despite exceptions there has been little long lasting gain for many local communities - black or white - in terms of strategies which genuinely empower them, and little real pluralism. Even so, there has been some accumulation of pressures from the grass roots.

The development of policies is outlined in the second part of the chapter, where we include an evaluation in terms of five issues. A large literature is available, but we can refer directly to only a limited part of it. The aim is to sketch some general features and mention shifts over time rather than give a scholarly account. Again, the apparent disregard or lack of explicit targeting of ethnic minorities in much policy is noted. The assumption has often been that black people would benefit alongside white households, and policies have been supposedly 'neutral' in this sense. There has also been somewhat inadequate monitoring of outcomes. Urban policies have done little to build up democracy or empowerment (although there have been exceptions), little effective connection has been made with some other key policy areas affecting the social division of welfare, gains going to ethnic minorities have been uncertain, and universalistic approaches rather than pluralistic ones still dominate definition of needs. Nonetheless, there has been some political impact, with scope for mobilizations by local people in the context of programme mechanisms.

The third section of the chapter focusses directly on housing renewal. The argument is that the long history of interventions reveals a lack of provision for collective grass roots empowerment and an absence of thought about distributive impact; black people's gains are hard to measure, but may have been unimpressive. These characteristics - we will assert - are the very issues that are crucial to evaluating many of those other policies generally referred to in the term urban policies. On the other hand, some housing policies have helped inner city residents effectively, and this may have been feasible especially where there was

34

a link with individual or collective ownership, or where housing organizations developed a strong community orientation.

Having sketched the urban policy record, the chapter turns to possible causation. If urban policy has failed to accommodate pluralism and respond to demands for grass roots empowerment, the explanation may lie partly outside the sphere of explicit urban policy formation and implementation. One question to consider will be how far it has been possible to shift or amend the social division of welfare (described in chapter 2) in the urban context, in response to new groups' needs and the increased fragmentation of demands. The constraints under which urban policies have developed will be observed. In effect we tackle part of the roots of the urban policy situation by looking at the social policy record in a general way. Social policy has been restrained by paternalism, centralism, and economic liberalism, as well as by factors in the broader economic scene, notably public expenditure problems, economic decline and industrial restructuring. Its apparently universal provisions have been less neutral than might appear, and built around norms of respectability, culture, etc. In these circumstances there are enormous obstacles to any attempt from the grass roots to alter the social policy agenda or insert new demands. It would require major changes to shift the social division of welfare in directions which would help those inner city residents who are marginalised, materially or in terms of power.

The spatial division of welfare, ethnic diversity, and governmental responses

There is a *spatial division of welfare* as well as a social one. Consequently patterns of advantage and disadvantage for consumers may be found to have a complex locational geography as well as having links with broad features of social stratification. Alongside the impact of labour markets, infrastructure investment, and patterns of property investment, inheritance or related income, we must set the impact of social welfare services and support systems. There is some manifestation of stratification derived from the world of work and wealth, and reinforced or formed via the social division of welfare, in terms of segregation and differential patterns of consumption expressed geographically. The physical milieu may itself then exert some additional influence on opportunities and welfare for households. Some communities appear to fare rather badly as a result of these factors. Over time the pattern of relative welfare has been influenced by differential industrial and commercial growth and decline, which appears to have worked against many inner city populations.

It is unlikely that relative deprivations are all tightly concentrated in geographical terms in a simple sense, but for several decades UK central governments have been concerned that inner city areas appeared to contain large numbers of people with difficulties of one sort or another (for issues of definition, etc., for areas of deprivation, see Eversley, 1992). Employment opportunities had been declining and numbers in relative poverty appeared to have grown, while mobile individual consumers and workers with the opportunity to choose had frequently moved out to preferred environments elsewhere (for a summary of some of the issues see Hausner and Robson, 1985). What is often thought of as the 'private' welfare sector - and notably those services which depend on credit ratings and estimates of relative risk - had taken an uncertain view of some inner areas.[2] This could give a strong spatial dimension to the well understood phenomenon that the poor may pay more than others do for equivalent services, goods and loans, or find difficulty in getting them at all (for comments see Williams, 1977). The inner city populations themselves had changed, with growing minority ethnic groups appearing increasingly significant for public policy, and with a considerable diversity of cultures and needs. There are still large numbers of poor white households, including many who live on very low status council estates in extremely difficult conditions, but black people can face added problems of harassment, exclusion and racial discrimination. In the terms used by Rex they were not part of the welfare state 'deal' (Rex, 1986,pp.65-73), or the settlement of the 1940s and beyond, and we know that the process of incorporation through political channels (such as it is) is even today very incomplete (see chapter 4). None of this should be taken to imply homogeneous minority ethnic populations that are in some way universally 'trapped' in deteriorating inner city areas. There will be processes of 'exit' for successful individuals and groups that wish to move, although this might be held by some observers to be potentially debilitating for inner city communities.[3] Nonetheless, the overall pattern is one of continuing disadvantage and geographical concentration. As chapter 4 makes clear, there are important issues to do with segregation and lack of genuine choices here for many black people. We need to keep this in mind in the context of the deteriorated labour market position that has been facing many people in the inner areas.

The 'race' issue has not been solely a part of explicit urban policy, as it connects with other policy areas too, but the longstanding concentration of black people in specific geographical localities has linked 'race' and the urban in governmental consciousness. Various official responses to urban problems have reflected this. Recently the term 'settlement' (mentioned above in the context of the early post war years) has also been used to refer to UK 'liberal reforms in race policy of the 1960s' which helped shape 'the language and substance of race policy' (Saggar, 1993,p.33). As Saggar's account clearly indicates, however, the goals of this period were very much cast in broad public interest terms. We find little evidence of explicit attention paid to adjusting the boundaries of incorporation to bring black people into the most beneficial mainstream parts of the welfare state. It is even possible that broad targets, such as the goal of 'racial harmony', may be interpreted as having had as much to do with protecting the white majority from disturbance as assisting black communities. Some specific policies (such as dispersal strategies in housing allocation) have been very vulnerable to this kind of criticism. In any event, if there was a 1960s 'liberal settlement' underpinning British 'race politics', it did not shift the underlying characteristics of the social or spatial division of welfare, nor could it hope to do so except in the most peripheral way. Even within the directly provided public/social services sector, general perspectives continued to be rather unresponsive to cultural diversity and specific minority ethnic needs until relatively recently, while central government approaches strictly limited the amount of resources allocated explicitly to meet such needs. The role given to local government and local voluntary activity as key channels for securing integration and harmony was not supported by significant shifts in resources within mainstream programmes, taxation systems, etc., nor via adequate legal instruments.

On the other hand, there was development in political organization within ethnic minority communities, and some penetration of mainstream politics, as well as growth in independent and voluntary sector activity in the cities. Demands for better services, better representation, and recognition of the needs of cultural diversity, have been heard increasingly from black run organizations. This has been matched gradually by some resonances within urban services themselves, in terms of increased professional practitioner and management level awareness (perhaps particularly from the 1980s). These developments have been important in the housing field.

The development of 'urban' policies

It is in the context of a perceived inner city problem of which 'race' is a part that specifically designed 'urban' policies have operated since the late 1960s in the UK. A preoccupation with 'the cities' has been an important part of public policy debate. So much so that sometimes it is difficult not to get the impression that if inner cities could be erased then a host of social problems - 'underclasses', crime, deviance - would vanish overnight. This preoccupation is not confined to the UK, nor is it solely a concern of the second half of the twentieth century. There have always been observers who wished to redeem and sanitize 'darkest England' in the cities, from the nineteenth century onwards, and a strong tradition of anti-urbanism has been present in the UK from the time of the industrial revolution (for relevant material see Briggs, 1963; Coleman, 1973;

37

Stedman Jones, 1971). The problem that present day authoritarian politicians have is that transportation to the colonies is no longer available as a way of disposing of the recalcitrant poor, while prisons - although much admired as a solution - are an unfortunately expensive and (as recent events have proved) troublesome alternative. Governments have been faced with social conflicts and urban decline which have contributed to the accumulation of a complicated array of policies. Even since the Conservatives came to office in 1979 there has been a continuing commitment to remain involved through a range of strategies and expenditures. A question that has to be asked, however, concerns the usefulness of the policies from the point of view of marginalised communities. In particular, we need to reflect on how useful or empowering policies have been for black minority ethnic groups. We have already noted that general public interest goals such as securing harmony and integration may be interpreted as having been beneficial for white as much as for black people. It is necessary, though, to look more closely at the urban policy record.

We will start with a sketch of policy trends over the post war period and then turn to evaluation.[4] Sadly, although quite large sums have been spent in the cause of urban regeneration, there has been little effective monitoring either of the distributional impact of programmes or the consequences for local empowerment. This is not accidental, but reflects the character of urban policy, which has neither sought to address poverty directly, nor (as we have already noted) consistently prioritized needs and development for specific minority ethnic groups. The lack of effective monitoring means that our observations are in the form of an overview rather than a set of references to extensive data with a bearing on our concerns. This does not mean that central and local government departments have not tried to measure performance, but the types of outputs and results covered have not been sufficiently comprehensive or illuminating. There have been interesting review or monitoring projects sponsored by central government (for instance Public Sector Management Research Unit, 1985), and recently a weighty study by Robson et al.(1994). The latter has produced a mixed picture from its outcome measures (see p.viii,etc.), but some indicators appear to show worsening problems. Referring to findings in three selected conurbations, the study points to unemployment becoming spatially more concentrated over time, and to 'increasing polarisation' (p.ix).[5] Despite valuable research such as this report, however, it remains difficult to find reliable data measuring the broad impacts of urban policies on 'race' relations, community development and empowerment, or the welfare and prospects of minority ethnic people. To some extent this is understandable because of the measurement problems involved by comparison with 'straightforward' issues like unemployment, but there are also political reasons.

By contrast with the inadequacy of official monitoring there has been a regular flow of interesting accounts, essays and interpretations of policy and urban conditions from scholars. Examples (some of which are very well known) include Edwards and Batley (1978); Hambleton (1977); Higgins, Deakin, Edwards and Wicks (1983); Williams (1983); Stewart (1987 and 1994); Jacobs (1986 and 1992); Ratcliffe (1992); Sills, Taylor and Golding (1988); Lawless (1989); Munt (1994); Atkinson and Moon (1994); and Jones and Lansley (1995). There have also been numerous more technical or tightly focussed studies and reports (for instance Whitting, 1985; Memon, 1988; Stewart and Whitting, 1983; Ball, 1988; Aldridge and Brotherton, 1987; Harrison, 1989), while writers on topics such as planning or 'race' have sometimes addressed inner city questions within their books or papers (a good example being Smith, 1989). The present chapter does not attempt a systematic literature review, since we are now only concerned to give a very basic and simplified outline of events, but the section below has been strongly influenced by Stewart in particular.

Stages in policy development

Urban policy has always been made up of different sets of initiatives 'unevenly tacked together', so that to talk about successive 'paradigm shifts' can mean drawing 'excessively sharp distinctions between policies that coexisted over the whole period' (Deakin, 1995,p.44). Nonetheless, some leading writers on urban policy usefully identify a series of stages or phases through which British (or English) strategies have developed. Stewart, for instance, refers to 'a fitful succession of discontinuous initiatives', and says that urban policy 'has evolved since 1945 through a number of distinct stages' (1994,p.133). This is a very reasonable observation, and based on a detailed analysis of events, although subject to the qualification about not drawing excessively sharp distinctions between phases or policies. Caution must also be exercised, however, over just what we mean when we refer to urban policy. Sometimes a degree of compartmentalism is needed in order to discuss policies, although unrealistic if we want to understand the full range of relevant expenditures and programmes. So-called 'main programmes' or mainstream programmes can be referred to or left out by writers, depending on the direction of the discussion. For present purposes we will be including the explicit urban policies pursued by government since the late 1960s (initially largely as separate additions to the policy agenda), but also urban renewal policies for housing that have a longer history (dealt with separately below). We will not enter the debates about what constitutes or defines urban areas, or comment on the limitations of area based policies as such (which have generated critical comment from many authors over the years). Stewart's account of successive stages is accepted, but this will be supplemented by an assertion of the longstanding continuity of some elements of urban housing policy, or at least of the ideologies which have sustained them. It should be noted that government itself has run programmes with relevance for the inner cities under many headings and within various departmental compartments. Efforts at better co-ordination have been made from time to time, but governmental approaches may contain or conceal ambiguities over what ought to be included under the heading of 'urban strategy' or policy for the cities.

Stewart (1994,pp.133,etc.) describes the 'shoal of initiatives' of the 1960s by referring to a period of 'ameliorative social pathology built on an analysis of deprivation, social and economic isolation', and 'incorporating a community development philosophy aiming to integrate alienated urban populations' (including recent immigrants). How far a genuine community development philosophy made inroads into the then practices of local government and into the new programmes is a moot point. In this early period there was probably a mixture of motives and causes. Perhaps we should partly think in terms of emergency actions derived from or reacting to a kind of moral panic over racism and potential urban conflicts; Stewart says that 'Fear of racial tension has always been at the heart of urban policy' (1987,p.132). In addition there was a view that social conditions of multiple deprivation were concentrated in specific areas where supportive actions could be focussed selectively, through adjustments to educational budgets, or via support for community development initiatives or voluntary agency interventions. Expenditure levels were low at this time. Interestingly, perhaps one of the initiatives which sat most uneasily alongside conventional services and political preferences was the one most directly confronting questions of community development, and (potentially) empowerment; the Community Development Project (for an account of the CDP see Higgins, Deakin, Edwards and Wicks, 1983).

A major shift in policy direction came with the increasing acceptance of economic and structural explanations of relative urban decline (see especially Secretaries of State for the Environment, Scotland and Wales, 1977). Although social welfare concerns remained on the agenda during Labour's period in office, 1978 legislation recast intervention to reflect the challenges of unemployment, job creation, and local economic policy pursued through a partnership of central and local government (see Inner Urban Areas Act, 1978). Since this watershed the primacy of economic considerations has not really been challenged, but the balance between key participants has altered over time.

Conservative governments have confirmed their public commitment to the inner cities in various ways (see for example Cabinet Office, 1988), but strategies have been influenced by the desires to bring in private capital and cut or restrain certain public expenditures, as well as to highlight issues like crime prevention (see for instance Home Office, 1992). The post-1979 period was also characterized by changing central/local government relations leading to reduced roles and influence for local authorities. This is a backcloth against which urban policy needs to be set.

In the development of urban policy the next phase to emerge was, as Stewart puts it, one 'predicated ... on a strategy of physical regeneration which drew in major financial resources from the private sector, used public expenditure as the leverage for property led urban regeneration, and featured new institutions and instruments of policy such as Urban Development Corporations and Urban Development Grant' (1994,p.134). Much of the activity of this period has been denounced by independent critics, despite the large sums going into some programmes. The diversion of major shares of funding into the hands of new unelected QUANGOs at the expense of local democratic control, the depth and style of co-operation with major private commercial interests, and the stress on 'property-led' regeneration (meaning market orientated reconstruction and infrastructure spending), have drawn some savage fire from scholars (an interesting example is Ambrose, 1986,chapter 8,etc.). Stewart says that this phase of policy 'rose and fell with the property cycle of the late 1980s' (p.134), and has been superseded by 'some reconciliation' or perhaps a 'forced truce' between central and local government - allowing the emergence of an era of 'collaborative partnership' between levels of government and public and private sectors. He notes an emphasis on the incorporation of a wider range of interests into policy implementation, and an explicit competition over the allocation of resources. We should not forget, however, that non elected bodies still control huge areas of economic and social life, and that this managerial system has been an area of considerable agency growth in the period since 1979 as far as delivery of local services is concerned. There is great variety and inconsistency in the ways in which QUANGOs are governed, and lack of clarity about accountability (JRF, 1994a). Meanwhile, local authorities have been expected to move towards becoming enablers rather than direct suppliers in some spheres, while the competitive practices into which they have been pushed can include bidding for specific budget funds in ways which may downgrade the significance of relative need.

Most recently there have been moves which appear to address some of the problems of fragmentation and compartmentalism (that have characterized central government's approach), with the setting up of a new 'Single Regeneration Budget' (SRB) system to be run through integrated regional offices. From April 1994 twenty targeted programmes, including specific urban and housing programmes, were to be brought together in this system, supporting regeneration and economic development. It is too early to know the full implications of this change, but some interesting critical observations have already been offered by Shiner (see 1995 [6]). Analysing the outcomes of the first

41

round of the SRB competition, he suggests that government has disguised 'substantial reductions in funding for urban regeneration', and he goes on to draw attention to five major criticisms. These relate to lack of accountability and dangers of patronage, issues of social equity, inefficiency, a threat to housing capital programmes, and his view that the SRB 'is a scam' (providing a cloak for dramatic reductions in projects, etc.). For our purposes it is worth noting that Shiner sees the problems of 'concentrations of socially excluded groups in urban areas' worsening, while feeling that the omission of certain deprived areas with large minority ethnic populations from the list of successful bids raises questions about government's commitment to equal opportunities.

Finally, we need to add the point that there is now a 'European dimension' to inner city regeneration, and that European programmes may have some impact in UK settings (Atkinson and Moon, 1994). Moore indicates that the problem of racism has been put on the agenda at the European level, 'although with difficulty' (1995,pp.162-3), and that - amongst other things - the Third Poverty Programme seeks to secure participation 'with the most excluded groups'.

A general evaluation of policy impact and characteristics

Evaluations of inner city or urban policies have been pursued by independent scholars, carried out from local authority level, and commissioned by central government (see literature cited above). There are a number of conclusions that can be drawn from looking back over the history. These fall into five broad (overlapping) areas of concern.

First, in terms of frameworks for democracy and empowerment there has been very little to benefit local communities. Indeed a certain amount has probably been lost rather than gained. Stewart mentions the 'relentless centralisation of management and control' (1994,p.134) that has occurred. Despite any rhetoric about community development, collaboration, partnership or pluralism, much innovation has relied on establishing ad hoc agencies, appointed teams and QUANGOS. In the context of so called partnerships, the officially sponsored report by Robson et al.(1994) observes that local communities might have played a role in local coalitions, 'but it has generally not been a high priority of government policy to develop such community participation in the 1980s and this is seen by many as a missed opportunity' (p.xiii). With regard to the City Challenge programme, a Rowntree Foundation study comments that attempts to involve the community have had 'patchy results', and community input into the initial strategic planning stage for producing plans was low (JRF, 1994b). More generally, the approach to urban policies has 'diluted the impact of locality based structures of power and influence, most notably the power of elected local government' (Stewart, 1994,p.135). Many physical changes have been pressed

42

upon local areas without any genuine consultation. The latest central government steps - with their new regional emphasis - may turn out to be more in the direction of creating an additional level in a new 'squirearchy' than a genuine devolution of power to localities (although for a range of possible interpretations see Stewart, 1994,pp.142-4). Despite this overall picture, certain parts of the urban policy package have been more amenable to democratic pressures or to the empowerment of particular local groups, voluntary bodies or community interests. This responsiveness was to an extent implicit during the earliest period of intervention, when the programmes had a 'social' slant, but has remained a factor throughout where expenditure has retained a social welfare or community development dimension. For much of the time, however, economic, commercial and environmental concerns have had higher priority. Apparently, the government's central aim in recent years has been to promote economic and physical regeneration, and encourage economic development and industrial competitiveness. Expenditures which can lever in private sector investment may be preferred, even though 'leverage discriminates against projects which do not appeal to private sponsors' (Shiner, 1995). The process of community development through creating and strengthening local participatory channels for residents has been far less emphasized.

A *second* point is that very little explicit connection has been made (or acknowledged) by government between certain of its strategies affecting the social division of welfare on the one hand (see chapter 2), and the continuation of inner area problems on the other. This does not imply that ministers have failed to recognise the significance of established mainstream policies and programmes, since the need to give these an inner city dimension has been stated from time to time (see for instance Higgins, Deakin, Edwards and Wicks, 1983,p.125). Even though there has been little evidence of genuine and consistent enlargement or 'bending' of some main expenditure programmes in the interests of the poor, at least the necessity has sometimes been accepted at the level of rhetoric or general intent. Indeed, it can be argued that at least in housing policy the idea of identifying stress areas geographically, and using needs indicators, has influenced investment patterns significantly.[7] In addition there have been specific ad hoc programmes for estate revitalization, etc. Unfortunately, such methodologies can be undermined by cuts in investment levels or shifts in the orientation of programmes to meet other political criteria (such as bringing in private capital, or boosting owner occupation through a programme for shared ownership).

What is more significant, however, is the longstanding pursuit of goals in certain policy areas in ways which may have worsened matters severely but less visibly in the inner city. The impact of taxation measures, privatization and employment policies, and general strategies on deregulation, competition, local

43

government, public expenditure and benefits, may have been working against many inner city residents over much of the last fifteen years. This tendency, and the property focus of many policies in the 1980s, are central reasons for limitations in the beneficial impact of urban policies on social life (cf Smith's conclusions, 1989,p.74, and Lawless, 1989,pp.148-51,167,etc.). The result is that as Sills, Taylor and Golding put it in 1988, the scale of urban poverty 'continues to dwarf and outrun the level of urban programmes by a factor which calls into real doubt the extent to which these programmes are seriously intended to tackle the roots of the problem' (p.166). Even infrastructure spending which appears as part of the regeneration effort for an urban area can work against certain disadvantaged categories of residents. (We noted in chapter 2 the possibilities for transport spending having regressive distributional - and health - affects.) In effect any attention paid to prioritizing the urban disadvantaged cannot be said to have much offset factors working against them over the same period, let alone made substantial favourable amendments to their position in the social division of welfare. Central government rhetoric denies or ignores this.

Thirdly, if we look at the benefits going to minority ethnic groups there is uncertainty over gains, and few data. Even within the relatively socially orientated parts of the package there has been only a limited gain in terms of opportunities to have control of, create, or manage, substantial investments, enterprises or services. Despite the significance of 'race' at the time the programmes began in the 1960s, targets and planning have been largely in 'neutral' terms (not specifically tied to minority ethnic needs, but to the inner cities in general), and monitoring has been weak (Harrison, 1989). It is difficult to demonstrate that there has been either a large flow of direct benefits or an effective 'trickle down' process which has helped minority ethnic communities (see Ratcliffe, 1992). Of course this is not necessarily very different from the situation for many white inner city residents. Certainly it has been argued that regeneration efforts concentrated on central area property orientated strategies have led to the concept of 'two speed' cities, where the renewal of the urban core is juxtaposed with the continued decline of neighbourhoods dependent on traditional employment (see JRF, 1993b; Thake and Staubach, 1993). No doubt both black and white people have lost out through this effect. Yet it has frequently been implicit that at least minority ethnic communities must be benefiting, even though no clear mechanisms existed to produce that result. In commenting on 'curious and well-known aspects' of certain policies, including various urban aid initiatives, Bulpitt asserts that anti-deprivation programmes were 'not explicitly designed to help blacks'. As he puts it, it was constantly emphasized that all citizens in the relevant districts were expected to benefit (1986,p.33). In these circumstances it would be very interesting to have more

44

data on who has (or has not) been helped over the last three decades, since many people at grass roots seem to feel that black communities have 'lost out'.

There are of course examples of valued projects for minority ethnic community groups and organizations; some black run voluntary organizations certainly have been assisted. In addition a certain amount of expenditure has been allocated to help deal with problems such as harassment, which directly affect these communities (for instance see Home Office, 1992, p.5). On the other hand these things seem to have been modest in cost terms for government, even if only looked at in terms of the share taken of the budgets for explicit urban policy. Some of the projects have been vulnerable to cuts and withdrawals of funding, and their precariousness has contrasted with the more established services focussed through universalistic channels. Voluntary sector involvement has also given opportunities for established white run bodies to shape agendas and pre-empt funds. Dependency of black groups on larger white run partners, or as clients for short term discretionary departmental funding, has been a recognized outcome. On the small businesses front there have been positive examples of progress in which voluntary organizations, local authorities and other official agencies have played a part. There has been an ethnic minority business initiative, and grant available to encourage employment, training and enterprise projects run by voluntary organizations. As far as sharing in the indirect benefits of capital investment goes, however, there is virtually no systematic evidence that the large volume expenditures on property development, purchasing, and infrastructure work have systematically fed the sustained growth of local black run businesses (a matter we will return to in chapter 6). We should remember the big difference there is between ad hoc promotional, supportive and training exercises on the one hand, and a share in the regular contract expenditures initiated or enabled by public agencies on the other.

Summarizing, we can say that there has been scope for black led social, business, and community organizations to develop or mobilize around some programmes, but this has remained marginal for government budgets in financial terms. By contrast, there has probably been little beneficial impact for black communities as far as the destinations of the profits and other 'spin offs' from inner area capital investments have been concerned. Meanwhile, resources for staffing that are beneficial for ethnic minority communities have tended to be short term in the context of time-limited social projects.

Fourthly, despite increasing understanding of cultural pluralism, there has been a continuing tendency for universalistic notions to dominate the defining of needs, and this has been taking some time to diminish. Cultural or ethnic divergences have not yet been fully matched by diversity in agency responses, especially within long established mainstream programmes which have proved difficult to 'bend'. Targeted urban programmes have helped in some ways, since

45

innovation has occurred via expenditures that have fallen outside traditional mainstream channels. Even so, surprisingly few elements of this expenditure have been harnessed openly to needs defined specifically in terms of ethnic minorities, although Section 11 monies could be interpreted in this light (see Local Government Act 1966, S.11 and Local Government [Amendment] Act 1993; Home Office, 1988; and Ratcliffe, 1992,p.389 for comment), and there have been community centres and other support provided for specified groups in some places. On the other hand - despite the adherence to universalistic notions of service provision - there has often been no genuinely universal access to resources on an equal basis.

Fifthly, we do need to note that in some places increased awareness and more open networks of contacts may have been brought about partly through urban policies and their influence on main programmes and the voluntary sector. In effect the array of programmes has had a variety of local political consequences over the years. This may have influenced the capacity and preparedness of potential beneficiaries to mobilize, in a context where there are urban policies that could attract concern, approval or local struggles. On the local authority side there has been recognition that managing certain programmes produced new networks of contacts with residents, the organized voluntary sector and the private sector (see Aldridge and Brotherton, 1987,p.366). Also, awareness of support systems may have increased among previously excluded groups via a generation of experienced activists. Local limits have existed, though, given the tight constraints on practice. An agency may be either an outpost of central government taking its lead from ministers, or grafted onto the local government system with its white dominated councillor and officer structure, and trade unions. Sometimes the rhetoric of participation or partnership can hide divisive processes of competition for funds, the 'strangling' of dissidents and community protest 'by red tape and failure', and political patronage targeting resources 'to key opinion leaders or groups rather than to the needs of the communities they claim to represent' (see Sills, Taylor and Golding, 1988,p.163). Additional comments on the political issues follow in the next chapter, with particular reference to minority ethnic groups and their housing.

Housing renewal; similar characteristics?

It is difficult to summarize the impact of governmental housing strategies affecting the inner cities, so our commentary is selective. Nonetheless we will refer to renewal traditions, help for owner-occupiers, and new build.

During the late 1960s there was a break with earlier outlooks, as government focussed on the apparent decline and social problems of inner cities, instead of simply continuing the physical reconstruction and decentralization planning that had followed the war. At the same time the emphasis came off large scale demolition projects within urban housing, and shifted towards rehabilitation of old dwellings (for a good history see Gibson and Langstaff, 1982). Yet although the 'reconstruction era' of massive slum clearance programmes was drawing to a close by the early 1970s, there was a degree of continuity in housing renewal practices which linked past and present. Even today the legacy of past outlooks and methodologies is important.

The physical improvement tradition

Physical intervention in the quality of housing provision in Britain had its roots in the 'sanitary' school of the nineteenth century. The goal of tackling slums had very strong public health connections. It was linked with standard setting for new dwellings. Better dwelling and environmental standards, good sanitation, and access to light and air, were desirable goals that were expected to benefit residents and the wider community. State funds and agencies had a clear role to play. We can see this approach as having fitted well both with Tory paternalism, and with the reform and planning themes of Fabian social engineering. The sanitary tradition operated strongly in the 1930s era of clearance, and from the 1940s to the 1960s. It has survived in the context of housing improvement grants and area policies, as well as in such slum clearance as still occurs. Central to the tradition, however, has been an emphasis on physical change rather than the measurable social welfare or the cultural orientations of specific resident households. Until the recent advent of means tests on grants, it might have been hard to argue that the programme had even really targeted the poorest directly, but easy to claim that it served objectives of a more general kind. Goals were 'public interest' ones, defined as such from paternalistic governmental perspectives rather than from grass roots visions. Although improving the physical environment might help secure environmental quality for old housing areas, this could sometimes bring as much joy to evangelistic administrators as to poorer residents whose housing costs and household budgets might be adversely affected (relevant studies include Dennis, 1970; McKie, 1971; Davies, 1972). In some times and places there was scant regard paid to local communities, and the differences of outlook, needs or culture that might be found within and between them. At the same time housing renewal was sometimes pursued without much effort at linking housing strategies or needs with certain other influences affecting welfare; such as income, taxation and employment policies, or transport trends and costs.

This is not to deny the benefits households might gain, or the fact that slum clearance and improvement sometimes were capable of meeting residents' aspirations. It is simply that the distributional impacts for households were not necessarily the most serious concerns of government over most of the period, and that policies were imposed largely from above. If housing renewal has remained the most longlived and constant aspect of 'urban' regeneration policy, then perhaps that is not unconnected with the facts that it was primarily a physical strategy rather than a redistributional one, and that it conferred very little power over resources on local residents. Even today renewal and its side effects can sometimes appear very disruptive for householders (see for instance Courtney, 1993).

In recent years there has been a strong emphasis on regenerating older social rented housing estates, mixing physical and community development goals in the context of concentrated efforts backed by expenditure packages (in some instances bid for competitively from central government). This kind of renewal cannot necessarily much change the underlying socioeconomic forces producing disadvantage and disempowerment among residents (see chapter 2), but at least participation and tenant consultation have been part of the agenda in a way very different from some of the clearance enterprises of past times.[8]

Empowering owner-occupiers

Our line of argument about lack of power over resources needs qualifying with reference to the period from the late 1960s onwards, and to an extent in respect of improvement grants in general. The improvement of owner-occupied properties could offer at least a measure of empowerment, provided it was not financially or in other ways disruptive for a household. By the early 1970s there was an explicit intention to recognize social goals more directly in renewal practice (although perhaps there were tensions between social, managerial and physical goals inherent in the concept of Housing Action Areas). Furthermore, public participation began to enter the vocabulary of urban renewal during the 1960s, although it did not usually offer much direct control over investment options beyond the level of individual house owners making a yes or no decision on their dwellings. Where participation had most meaning as a collective process may have been where homeowners needed to be motivated to engage with area improvement strategies; in effect participation here was partly an adjunct to the growth or encouragement of an owner-occupier group in inner areas. At its best, perhaps the process gave these owners a chance to upgrade areas they had bought within. In recent years help has been extended further, in terms of 'care and repair', so that older people in need can receive advice and support in dealing with their homes. For tenants, improvement policies have also sometimes been helpful, but this might be dependent on landlords, security of tenure, etc., and tenants have sometimes been displaced during processes of upgrading or 'gentrification', or found their position changed significantly by alterations in tenancy laws.

The encouragement given to owner-occupiers since the demise of large scale clearance has had limitations, and the future of 'downmarket' owner-occupation remains unclear. There are claims that increasing numbers of people will need help in future, or that housing renewal policy in its most recent phase lacks sufficient awareness of the need to sustain ongoing maintenance in inner city owner-occupied dwellings. (See Leather and Mackintosh, 1993, for a good discussion of issues.) Even so, the support given to owners through improvement policy has been one of the elements in urban policy that has contained a demonstrable 'empowerment component' for households. Whereas clearance undermined independent owner-occupation, improvement was capable of strengthening it. This has not been parallelled by anything equivalent, conferring control of resources on a more collective basis, except in the relatively small scale area of co-op housing renewal, although housing associations involved in rehab. schemes have often had strong community orientations. The co-op movement has been innovative, and significant in a number of cities, but has made minimal inroads on the public purse. It is important to note that collective or individual property ownership seems to be one key to the state offering residents a genuine type of empowerment in the renewal process.

Modern new build programmes and local gains

New build need not be linked with clearance, and it is necessary to add some comments on the impact of urban local authority and housing association new build programmes to supplement remarks so far. It is clear that there has been no certainty over the years that the most needy would benefit through social rented housing allocation processes and the prioritizing of schemes (see our next chapter). Also, although government agencies have rationed or guided main programme expenditure in ways that have sometimes emphasized disadvantaged areas, these big spending programmes have been vulnerable to political or ideological changes at governmental level, and subject to cuts or competition for funding. Nevertheless there have been some efforts at involving communities through local authority participation processes and through housing associations linked with localities or specific needs. The most relevant example for present purposes is the Housing Corporation's programme for black and minority ethnic housing associations, which is referred to in chapter 5. These developments have contained the possibility of a measure of group or collective empowerment in the processes of urban renewal, although - as with improvement for owner-occupiers - there have been limitations.

A key ideological feature of housing renewal has been a concept of change seen paternalistically in terms of physical planning and standards. Indeed it could be argued that even some of the forms of empowerment acknowledged above are best seen as byproducts of an essentially physical environmental approach. The target was to upgrade the cities. To suggest that the supposed gains in welfare should have been systematically compared with what might have been achieved by letting residents spend the money for themselves on whatever they felt most useful would have been regarded as outrageous. Yet the beneficial nature of higher environmental standards was not always easy to prove. Even with health goals - one of the most acceptable bases for paternalism - it was hard to demonstrate unequivocally that residents actually benefited from higher standards, since so many other potential causative variables were involved. At the same time there has never been an assumption that the beneficiaries of the employment generated by renewal monies should be drawn from the inner city areas. Today housing renewal strategy lags behind social change, and sidesteps crucial issues of welfare and need which may undermine the prospects of sustained physical improvement. For improvement policy has not yet come to terms with the 'downmarket' extension of owner-occupation and the support that would be needed to give poorer consumers the full benefits of this form of ownership. At the moment the experience of owner-occupation is a very differentiated one, and it is far more empowering to better off than to poorer households. Urban renewal for tenants may promise some immediate gains in quality of dwellings, but this must be set against questions about affordability, control, security, and access. Genuine and sustained collective empowerment through the process of urban renewal has not been very common. As far as minority ethnic groups are concerned, renewal (including new build in the inner areas) has become more sensitive to cultural variation, and there are examples of participation, but again the overall picture has been unimpressive. The question of whether black people benefit from the building contracts generated in the areas they reside in has rarely been on the official agenda.

The above discussion of housing renewal history complements our earlier commentary on UK 'urban policy', and there are parallels. Insofar as 'mainstream' urban renewal housing laws encouraged prioritization of particular localities and the tackling of urban decay, they were likely to align with the explicit urban interventions developed outside main programmes. The longer history on the housing side reveals a lack of developed formal frameworks for collective grass roots empowerment, a lack of concern for cultural diversity or for taking full account of other parts of the welfare state, and an absence of thought about distributive impacts. These are the very issues which are crucial to an evaluation of those 'bolt on' policies usually taken to constitute the core of explicit urban policy. On the other hand - again as elsewhere in urban policy - there has been scope for emergence of a politics of grass roots representation. There have also been some interesting possibilities of enhancing people's power over their dwellings where policies have linked up with property ownership by residents (collective or individual). This too finds a parallel in other urban policy, where local groups have acquired facilities such as buildings for community centres, etc. Finally, as far as minority ethnic groups have been concerned, lack of explicit monitoring - as in other areas of urban policy - has sometimes made it hard to see the extent of their gains from housing renewal (see for instance Ratcliffe, 1992,p.393),[9] but there has been some evidence of their losing out in investment. Furthermore, as Ratcliffe notes, it is not only whether improvements are carried out but who does them which is important (p.397). For most places governmental and other agencies have virtually no data on the distributional impact of contracts from the point of view of black firms.

The constraints and ideologies of social policy, and their role in the 'failure' of urban policy

The paragraphs above have noted the limitations of urban strategies as channels for assisting and empowering black and minority ethnic communities and households, in the context of the general failure of urban policies to substantially adjust patterns of relative disadvantage and advantage, or to create participatory channels. We will now conclude by summarizing the restraints operating in UK social policy, which have set boundaries around what could be achieved readily in urban policies. Some have been touched on already. The constraints we refer to may be summarized as follows:-

(a) The dominance of economic liberalism
(b) Economic decline and public expenditure constraints
(c) The centralizing and paternalistic traditions of governmental social policy
(d) Reluctance to accept diversity of aspirations, needs and culture
(e) Reluctance to acknowledge or confront the distributional effects of those public policies that are not focussed on aiding the marginalised

Especially since 1979, ideas derived from *economic liberalism* have carried much weight with government. Economic liberalism emphasizes decision making by individuals in situations of market choice, and downgrades the worth of many group or community forms of empowerment, eroding some kinds of collective bodies standing between the state and the individual (see for instance discussion

51

in Bowles and Gintis, 1986, pp.176-7,etc.). Economic liberals who favour free markets prefer subsidies to be given selectively to meet tightly specified individual needs (rather than to collectivities which might decide on use), and to feed into market style arrangements if possible. At the same time ideologies about incentives, the deserving, and the less deserving, imply that selective assistance for the poor should be seen not as an entitlement but a gift from the better off. The terms under which such a 'gift' are given will tend to restrict the degree of control the recipient has over it or its capital value. The client may even be expected to modify his or her behaviour, or to accept 'therapy' of some kind (retraining, treatment, 'workfare', regular contact with officials, etc.). Consequently expenditures to combat urban deprivation within an economic liberal framework cannot necessarily be expected to confer much power over resources. Where a group or voluntary body does gain access to funds the use may be strictly controlled. This may mean that monies are compartmentalized in ways which do not suit a local community, or that limits are set on local control of the indirect benefits (such as any contracts awarded as a result of a subsidy). The application of principles such as open competitive tendering might be required in some circumstances. Full privatization of service provision or management is preferred by economic liberals to local political or community control; making collective participation unacceptable, and outlawing any local politics aimed at redistribution or compensation for the weak. Potentially redistributive issues of any scale tend to be drawn into the central governmental level, leaving local influence confined to much more marginal decisions. Local authorities with Conservative leanings may be 'commodifiers' (Clapham, 1993,pp.35-7) as far as service provision goes, preferring to deal with individuals as isolated consumers rather than groups.

Economic decline and restructuring in labour markets has enhanced economic liberalism's grip on public policy; through the reduction of the political strength of organized labour which has accompanied industrial change, and through the pressure that resource restraints have put on direct provision of public services. It has been possible to press for *public expenditure constraints* and a bigger share of activity for private capital on the grounds that this is not only desirable but also essential for economic health. This has stimulated the selling off of public assets such as land or houses (often cheaply), the emergence of 'partnerships' between private and public sectors, the creation of private franchises and semi-monopoly situations in place of direct public ownership, and the by-passing of local electoral channels in favour of QUANGOS which will relate more satisfactorily and compliantly to private capital's needs. In such circumstances minority ethnic groups may have been losing opportunities for present and future access to services and resources. It would be interesting to have data on the direct financial beneficiaries of privatization and so forth; they

52

are mostly likely to be people and companies based well outside the inner cities. If the party is over, the latecomer will find little food or drink left!

The centralizing and paternalistic traditions are probably as strong as economic liberalism in UK social policy, and have taken on renewed force through central government's increasing monopoly of power in the 1980s and 1990s. UK social policy is primarily a national level phenomenon, restricted by powerful interests and electoral considerations that press upon and through the political parties, especially the Conservative Party. This does not preclude co-operation with outside interests, but genuine co-operation tends to be selective. Those welfare orientated organizations that in the past were accepted as potential informants or partners might themselves be infused with paternalistic outlooks and practices.[10] The continuing absence of levels of elected government at regional level (or in Scotland and Wales), has been reinforced by the increasing weakness and insecurity of local government; the situation in Britain perhaps lies at one extreme in terms of international comparisons among 'advanced' western societies (for some brief comparisons see JRF, 1994).

One consequence of centralization is that there can be a great deal of inertia in national politics, even though changes are taking place elsewhere. Even where local minority ethnic communities are very strong, for example, they have not yet secured major changes in resource distribution via local political successes. To some extent it could be argued that centralization is 'necessary' in order to protect - following what we said above - economic liberalism or the accumulation of profits, but that would be a rather deterministic view.[11] In any event, even if we wanted to think in terms of political dualism or a dual polity that implied some independence between central and local levels (see discussion in Saunders, 1986,pp.295-311; cf Bulpitt, 1986), we would have to accept that while peripheral issues may be delegated to locality level, real resource choices at that level are severely restricted in the UK. Local authorities did possess considerable influence, but their powers, autonomy and property have been sharply and rapidly eroded over the post-1979 period (see Cochrane, 1993, for interpretations). Sometimes this has been presented as reducing controls over the individual consumer, but there has been a strange mixture of recommodification, use of voluntary and non-elected forms of management, and a few selective new opportunities for collective participation (in education and housing).

One interpretation of changes might be to suggest that they have been opening up more diverse channels for meeting needs, and offer prospects for greater empowerment. Certainly some households have gained control of assets on an individual basis (as with the right for tenants to buy council houses), but there is a vacuum as far as more collective empowerment is concerned. The weight of tradition is important here. Although local government had previously secured a wider political pluralism than would have developed via central government on

53

its own, British local authorities had not been well adjusted to facilitating forms of local community controlled services. We have only to think of the record in urban housing renewal (noted above) to appreciate how poor local government had sometimes been in this respect. Given the absence of other types of devolution of power from central government, the UK has only very limited experience of community based management of services, involving users or consumers (either from a particular locality or with common needs). There is even less experience of consumers (or employees) having collective control over assets and their use. Even the UK's housing co-operatives movement is small scale, and has faced a commercial, financial and political environment that has presented obstacles rather than opportunities.[12] The absence of well developed systems for involving people collectively in day to day decisions has been a major feature of UK social policy. Social policy even disempowers people in some instances, particularly where a residual service is concerned (see chapter 2). Yet regularized local systems for genuinely empowering people would have been required if urban policy was to have taken adequate account of the increasing diversity of communities and households.

Given what we have observed about centralization and paternalism, it is unsurprising that social policy has rarely catered explicitly for diversity and minority needs. The centre and its ruling elites have been concerned with the mainstream, with integration of groups into the life styles of 'the respectables', and with satisfying the interests of powerful national constituencies. Attitudes to gypsies and travellers have illustrated most clearly the reluctance of governments to recognise the claim to be different and yet share in the resources of citizenship. Hostile attitudes to travellers are not unconnected with issues of power over land and property, which means that conflict is not simply the result of a moral panic among the 'respectable'. Perhaps material interests may often be involved in what appear to be clashes over culture or life style. Nonetheless, although there is still a *reluctance to accept diversity of aspirations, needs and culture*, some inroads have been made on this tradition in public policy and its implementation. Pressure from minority ethnic groups has clearly begun to erode some certainties about universality of needs and treatment. Moreover, English law and regulation have already had to deal with cultural or ethnic dimensions in many spheres; a scholarly account is given by Poulter (1986). Nevertheless, the machinery through which welfare is delivered remains poorly adapted to genuine pluralism.

Our last point in this chapter concerns central government's *reluctance to acknowledge the extent and character of the real welfare state*. This has had wide implications for the kinds of inner city policies that have been on offer. Perhaps this stance is part and parcel of the social division of welfare itself. After all, as we have been at pains to show in chapter 2, the social division of welfare concerns power as well as other kinds of resources. If the better off dominate the political system and public forum in which presentation and management of issues takes place, then perhaps we should expect their preoccupations to dominate also. One problem of this for inner city residents, however, may be that they are receiving a far smaller share of the benefits of state patronage than governments claim, yet this is obscured in much public discussion. Their difficulties are likely to be inadequately monitored, measured or evaluated at the technical level.[13] Even the assertion that many are experiencing forms of racist discrimination may be played down by ministers or officials. Academics and other independent observers do not have the excuse of a constituency that they must serve with a reaffirmation of comfortably misleading accounts. We should acknowledge that the UK welfare state in its paternalistic, centralized, and divisive form has not been tackling the 'urban problem' in a way that is even remotely effective, or genuinely empowering. This is despite some scattered exceptions. The continuing adverse experiences of ethnic minorities - to which we turn in the next chapter - provide plenty of evidence of this failure.

Notes

1. Some of the general policy orientated literature on 'race' and on the inner cities in the UK makes only limited distinctions between England, Scotland and Wales. Our account does not do justice to the distinctiveness of the three countries in policy terms, and some of the observations in the present chapter might need qualifying or adding to for Scotland in particular. This deficiency reflects our need to produce a fairly condensed general introduction to inner city policies, but also connects with the geographical limitations of the Leeds University research referred to in later chapters. See Lawless, 1989,pp.93-6 for an introduction on Wales and Scotland; also Atkinson and Moon, 1994,pp.158-9. See also Donnison and Middleton, 1987.
2. One recent press report captures vividly the problems still experienced by inner city householders in obtaining facilities; 'Insurers spurn inner cities', The Guardian, 25 March 1994.
3. Cf USA experience; see Wilson, 1991, pp.7-9.
4. For comments on evaluation see Lawless, 1989, pp.146-8.
5. Writing less formally, in the press, Robson has noted that the armoury of policies used to attack urban problems in the 1980s did include good ideas, and that the expenditure had some positive impact on the fortunes of big cities, but that these things did not help the vulnerable. He has also referred critically to the disappearance of Urban Programme money 'which has

played such a part in supporting so many innovative local voluntary bodies'. See The Guardian, 15 June 1994.

6. Although the present writer is drawing only on a fairly short press contribution here.

7. The Housing Corporation, for instance, operated an inner city enhancement policy; see Kearns, 1990, for comments.

8. For coverage of the Estate Action Initiative see Pinto, 1993.

9. Interestingly, the need for monitoring in the context of Housing Action Areas seems to have been acknowledged by the government at the outset; see Secretary of State for the Environment, 1975. There was an expectation then that the HAA programme would be relevant to the 'special needs of, amongst others, ethnic minorities', and a 'watch' needed to be kept to see that they - like other disadvantaged groups - did in practice benefit. The importance of channels of communications was noted, and of involving those living in stress areas or representing their interests in the action programmes (see p.5.)

10. For relevant comments in the context of a discussion of the politics of disability see Oliver and Zarb, 1989, p.224.

11. Such a perspective, however, does have merit in helping to remind us of one of the paradoxes of economic liberalism; that it is heavily authoritarian and judgemental when faced with possibilities of people wishing to choose or develop outside market mechanisms, while it yet talks the rhetoric of liberty and choice.

12. Perhaps the reason here is that co-ops have suited neither economic liberals (to whom they could represent socialism) nor local authority Labour politicians (themselves by no means always libertarian or unpaternalistic).

13. Apart from possibilities that official figures on issues like homelessness or unemployment can understate the full extent of problems, the UK now has some more basic data problems. Underestimation of inner area populations may be affecting local figures on numbers of households and allied characteristics, with perhaps quite large numbers of the poor becoming less visible. This could come to influence local census based assessments of need. Owen (1992,p.13) notes that the 1991 census was the first modern census to encounter significant non-cooperation, 'resulting in an undercount of 965 thousand'. Amongst relevant factors might be 'attempts to avoid registration for the Poll Tax'. See also an interesting paper by Simpson and Dorling, 1994, and various press reports (for instance 'Missing: two million of the UK's citizens' and 'One million missed in 1991 census', The Guardian, 6 January 1995).

4 Housing conditions, racism and consumer strategies

This chapter provides an overview of some general issues concerning ethnic minorities, as well as a selective survey of housing research literature and findings. We will begin with reminders of connections between urban deprivation, areas of settlement, labour markets, and ethnic divisions. It is important to recognize that preferences and strategies play significant roles alongside economic disadvantage. We will also include comment on the need to acknowledge diversity of experience within minority communities, while accepting the evidence that such communities face severe problems. Amongst these problems are concerns that are hard to quantify statistically, and we deal with some of these in a separate section: in particular we comment there on racism, segregation and citizenship. Then in later sections the chapter will turn more directly to housing conditions and the housing research record. Finally we discuss issues of housing politics, minority ethnic organization and action. A *key assumption* underlying the chapter *is that housing studies need to continue to take account of strategies pursued by groups, communities and individual households*. As in other chapters, the term community is used without specific theoretical connotations, as a convenience for descriptive purposes.[1]

Concentration, deprivation and preferences

It is important not to confuse notions of deprivation with the fact that minority ethnic populations are concentrated in particular localities. A concentration of black people in an area does not mean that there will necessarily be poverty or a sense of disadvantage there, nor is the presence of minority ethnic groups a *cause* of deprivation. Following arguments in earlier parts of this book, it should be clear that adverse inner city conditions cannot be understood by 'blaming victims' who may live there. Indeed, residents will not necessarily see

57

themselves as victims. We cannot assume in advance of empirical knowledge that they will be either satisfied or dissatisfied with living in a particular area. It is any restrictions and limitations that people face which may make living in a locality problematic for them. Furthermore, an outsider's perception of an area may be unrealistic for those who live there, and the tradition of focussing on 'problem areas' has led to some false ideas about the dangers of concentrations of people from particular backgrounds. In housing policy this may have contributed both to ideas of containment and involuntary dispersal of black communities.[2] The idea that concentration is a damaging process - produced by external forces, accident, or social pathologies - also may undervalue the importance of action and choice within minority communities.

In practice, geographical concentration actually can be advantageous for minority ethnic residents in some respects; in terms of security for households against racist attack, for political organization, for religious, educational or voluntary activity, to maintain family networks, to benefit from the presence of one's own linguistic group, or because of easier access to specialized cultural provision (religious, dietary, etc.). As Phillips puts it, the segregated ethnic neighbourhood may be seen 'as a separate territory, which serves to heighten and proclaim the distinctive identity of the minority, and provide support and protection for the immigrant' (1981,p.110; see also Habeebullah and Slater, 1990). That this is so might be borne out by any tendency for continuing geographical clustering of specific minority groups - for instance 'intra-community' segregation within Asian or African/Caribbean populations - although a variety of other factors may play a part in this.[3] The reputational character of an estate or district may be influential, and historical processes such as 'chain migration' can give a specific character to an area. Personal and family networks may pass on knowledge, and influence and facilitate decisions about moves within any migrant group. For example, in discussing Spitalfields in East London, Eade notes that the 'vast majority of Bengali settlers came from one particular district, Sylhet', and 'through the process of chain migration a substantial number appeared to come from particular villages or rural localities within Sylhet' (1989,p.27). The same study also observes that there was a greater 'pressure' among Bangladeshis than whites to live in Spitalfields. Certainly, although people's choices operate within economic and political limits, the role of preferences and community connections should not be overlooked when considering concentration, tenure and patterns of settlement at local level (see Rich, 1987,pp.77-8). This has long been recognized by researchers. As a Community Relations Commission study put it, nearly two decades ago, 'concentration is often voluntary' and 'some black people who live in ethnic concentrations have some very positive reasons for their choice' (Community Relations Commission, 1977,p.11). This does not preclude people having a preference for moving out of an area to better-quality accommodation elsewhere (and if they meet racist hostility then that may be a constraint which makes segregation partly involuntary). Nor does it deny that factors which 'bind people' to old housing neighbourhoods may 'exist alongside intense and growing frustration with housing conditions' (Habeebullah and Slater, 1990,p.1). The important point, however, is that the role of choice and individual action must be borne in mind. Households and groups may pursue strategies of their own, and should not be viewed as passive dependent variables.

Nonetheless, there are *associations* between material disadvantage and localities where non-white minority ethnic groups live in large numbers. It is important to understand what connects areas seen as disadvantaged with being from a minority ethnic group. This can be approached in rather specific empirical terms - in particular through looking at relationships to the world of work - or through considering racist processes of exclusion and segregation. We deal with these in turn below.

Links with the world of work

The primary connecting 'empirical' link is the position of groups in relation to labour markets, a connection that is complex and shifts over time, but remains an important source of differentiation. In discussing the origin and nature of urban deprivation Eversley states that 'the present position of the ethnic minorities within the inner cities is quite largely a matter of their involuntary involvement in the underlying changes in the fortunes of British industries.' (1992,p.148). Thus we can argue that black people have been disproportionately affected in adverse ways by industrial decline and restructuring. This must be set in detailed historical contexts. Present circumstances for many long established communities can still only be explained by looking at their specific histories, from the moment when members of the group were first drawn into the British labour market. Black workers initially often filled roles unacceptable to white people, and experienced negative discrimination and exploitation. Since then there has been a combination of disadvantages associated with concentration in particular industrial sectors and localities on the one hand, with barriers to upward or cross-sector movement on the other. Enterprise on the part of minority ethnic groups has been offset by their adverse position. Location in particular industries and at particular levels has made some groups vulnerable to unemployment, although job loss may often have much to do with a person's own insecure position. (Brown, 1992, gives a concise historical summary which brings out the complications.) Looking at today's scene, Jenkins notes the significance of discriminatory selection criteria and recruitment processes and the

59

disadvantaging impact of changes in 'the social processes of the labour market' (such as increased 'word of mouth' recruitment) (1992).

For new arrivals today - often relatively invisible by contrast with longer resident groups - the experience may be of marginalisation into work situations that are unhealthy, over-demanding and sometimes illegal. Detailed accounts of the 'new migrants' and their experiences remain unfortunately rare, although there are exceptions; the term slavery has been used to describe the worst excesses of employer behaviour (Anderson, 1993). For those who have lived here longer, and in many cases were born here, there may still be a discouraging overall pattern in the employment sphere. As Brown puts it, 'All the evidence suggests that there have been changes in the employment patterns of black and Asian people over the last decade, but that they are not converging with the employment patterns of whites, and that earlier injustices and imbalances continue to set the boundaries within which change can occur.' (1992,p.58). A weak position in the labour market tends to align with other kinds of disadvantage (as we noted in chapter 2), including low quality housing. Thus there are concentrations of black and minority ethnic households in areas suffering from high unemployment, poor housing, low car-ownership, and (in some cases) high proportions of rented property, with relatively large percentages of households lacking amenities and living at high densities (see Eversley, 1992,p.153). Some areas of minority ethnic residence may be unattractive to private corporate investors and represent a high risk for insurance purposes, but are also poorly served by types of provision in which state mediation on behalf of consumers has been more direct; for instance, they may be medically understaffed (Eversley, 1992,p.155).

While strong associations can be observed between labour market trends, conditions in disadvantaged districts, and ethnic minorities, there is a need for caution. Any over-simplified inner cities stereotype can be misleading. *Differentiation* exists between areas and among types of households. Changes in the distribution of employment opportunities over recent decades have been crucial to the declining status of inner areas, but generalization is difficult since variations between places and populations may be considerable. For instance, in a discussion of the 1971-81 period Hamnett and Randolph point out that the repercussions of labour market restructuring on the black workforce in London had not been felt uniformly; 'On the contrary, the distinctive variety of employment positions occupied by blacks... meant that restructuring ... worked its way unevenly through the black workforce, opening doors for some and closing them for others.' These repercussions had not all been negative, although 'it is quite clear that black workers in general ... fared less well than whites.' (p.204). These writers also state that 'Rather similar conclusions apply to the changing experience of blacks in the London housing market.' (1992,p.204).

Eversley notes the importance of differential experiences according to origins, places of initial settlement, educational and training experience, the industries in which they were originally employed, etc., rather than applying the label 'deprived ethnic minorities' without further qualification (1992,p.150). Nor can factors such as tenure be taken directly as easy identifiers of prosperity or lack of it. For instance, he continues, 'Some of the greatest poverty (and the worst overcrowding) occurs in ethnic minority households in owner-occupation, just as in the district of Knowsley in Merseyside some of the worst social and economic conditions occur in fit, purpose-built public sector housing.' (p.150).

Racism, conflict, segregation and citizenship

Associations between poor conditions and the geographical location of minority ethnic groups can also be considered (as we indicated above) by starting with racism. 'Racial' separation can be seen as something encouraged historically by the discriminatory practices of organizations, and maintained by pressures of racism operating at grass roots level. Some strategies adopted within minority ethnic communities - partly in response - may embrace avoidance of white localities and white run agencies, or stress independent action, in ways which consolidate separation.

There is a complex debate around the conceptualizing of race and racism charted within the literature on 'race' and ethnicity (see for instance discussions in Rattansi and Westwood, 1994; Miles, 1989; Solomos, 1993; Rex and Mason, 1986). Racism and notions of race can change over time, manifest themselves simultaneously in plural forms, and need to be understood in particular settings as well as in general terms. Racism need not be expressed only via an assertion of the significance of physical or biological differences, or as a hostility founded in a belief in the genetic superiority of one group over another. Culture may also be invoked in a racist perspective. Rattansi and Westwood (1994a,p.7) say there has been much debate in recent years concerning the degree to which the discrediting of nineteenth century doctrines of 'scientific racism' has 'given rise to racializing discourses that now rely on notions of cultural difference'. These discourses, they suggest, are 'new racisms' espoused by a variety of new right and neofascist organizations in Europe. Rattansi refers to a 'new politics of cultural difference' in western European societies (1994,p.23), but observes also that there has been disagreement about how new the 'new racism' itself might be (p.55). Certainly it could be difficult in looking at the past to disentangle views about 'race' in biological terms from hostile perspectives on culture and lifestyle, or from notions of national character not necessarily founded in supposed physical differences. In any event, in the UK some observers feel that

61

a 'new racism' has been emerging, in which the language of cultural division or deviation becomes a coded way of re-affirming white superiority or integrity within a discourse of 'belonging' (for discussion see Solomos and Back, 1994).

Clearly it is important to note any changes over time and in specific settings, bearing in mind that there are racisms rather than a 'singular racism' (Rattansi, 1994,p.57). As a parallel concern, we should acknowledge that cultural allegiances may play an enhanced political role within minority ethnic communities themselves. Thus we need to be alert to the possibility that a *politics of cultural difference* may include both racist and anti-racist movements, and that 'the saliency of "Black" as a unifying signifier' might have been 'losing its potency' (Rattansi, 1994,pp.67,75). Culture can be an important factor in relation to political identities and actions, alongside notions of colour or 'racial' division. We also need to be aware of the fact that overt biological racism may be bound up with more subtle expressions of hostility used to legitimate exclusion. Whether or not there has been a significant shift towards cultural issues in justifications used in social policy practice remains largely unmeasured. There is nothing new about criticisms of deviant lifestyles, less respectable categories, and outsider groups in social welfare fields (see chapter 2), and these have co-existed with racism in the past. Culture certainly has been inserted into housing practices as a basis for downgrading the claims of a black household for better accommodation. An excellent example is that revealed by Phillips; cooking smells that might be unacceptable to white households were cited as a reason for not allocating Asian households to desirable accommodation (Phillips, 1986,pp. 28,34). In any event we need to note cultural dimensions of racism and anti-racism, alongside more transparent expressions of racist hostility and more solidaristic forms of black resistance.

Racisms in practice

Racisms have frequently pervaded the operation both of private markets and public agencies in the UK, despite attempts to secure more equality of treatment through legislation. Positive efforts made by community relations agencies, and through developments towards good practice criteria in a number of fields, have been offset by lack of financial resources, limitations in the law, the implications for people living here of governmental strategies on immigration, and the continuing lack of powerful political channels open to minority ethnic constituencies. Whatever the relative importance of different causative factors, evidence of continuing discrimination is strong. An accumulation of research findings demonstrates that minorities may be treated adversely through institutional behaviour, as well as through individual and collective hostilities from white people at street level. Although welfare agency policies have frequently been formulated in neutral terms, they may not have been implemented in this way. Where there was an ideal of assimilation it might break down at the level of daily activity, where directly or indirectly racist institutional practices could sometimes find resonances in the views of local white residents.

In housing, discriminatory practices have contributed directly to spatial divisions along white/non-white lines. The segregation process can be interpreted partly in terms of a differentiated and complex structure of preferences, involving choices of white people as well as black. For instance, Eade's study of East London reports that, 'As in other urban areas of Britain with large concentrations of ethnic minorities', Bangladeshis 'appeared to be taking over space that white residents did not want or wanted less keenly than space elsewhere' (Eade, 1989,p.28). Studies generally suggest that spatial separation follows to an extent from the fact that white people have been able to choose more freely to move into better quality or - from their perspectives - higher status areas. For council housing, research studies cited later in this chapter have shown local authority housing departments sometimes heavily implicated in this process of 'racial' differentiation. Hostile reactions by whites to patterns of local socioeconomic change outside their control can mesh with the racism of housing officials.

In the social rented housing sector, opposition from white households may arise over allocations of tenancies to black people, but also over policy directions (see for instance Eade, 1989,pp.126,etc.). The situation in home and neighbourhood may be a base for this kind of explicit conflict more than the world of work, with housing being a crucial site of material struggles which become almost inextricably tied to 'racial' issues. The relative significance of social rented housing in an area, the supply and demand situation for it, and the degree of local dependence on it, may be factors contributing to the nature of local conflict. In situations of shortage of good quality provision there may be a receptive climate for institutional racism if local white residents see themselves as protecting their access to resources or their dominance of a locality. Even in the 1990s, effectively racist criteria have been evident in the formal rules adopted by some agencies. For instance, an agency may have prioritized demands for housing coming from 'sons and daughters' of existing residents of estates (see Eade, 1989,p.122; CRE, 1993,p.26; cf earlier periods, Burney, 1967,p.60). Some figures are available for one district in 1989-1991 from Ye-Myint (1992), suggesting that this practice overwhelmingly favours white applicants.

In some fields differential treatment of white and black people links up with stereotyping of minorities as the source of social problems or instabilities which threaten law and order (see Solomos, Findlay, Jones and Gilroy, 1982,pp.21-32; Solomos, 1988). Some may fare badly in encounters with the law and order system. One recent press report, for instance, cited a black MP as saying figures showed that the Metropolitan police were using stop-and-search powers to intimidate ethnic communities (the figures apparently having shown that over two fifths of Londoners questioned on the street by the police were black or Asian).[4] Yet at the same time some agencies remain complacent about breaches of law and order which victimize black people. Crimes of violence committed against minority ethnic people have been increasing in recent years, and constitute a major category of criminal activity. There is now quite a large literature on harassment and associated issues (see for instance Brown, 1984; Smith, 1989,pp.158-9; Smith with Hill, 1991,pp.21-23; Love and Kirby, 1994; Ginsburg, 1989). There can be a strong link with housing and competition for it, but the problem is not confined to areas of substantial minority ethnic settlement. Smith writes of the 'particular risks faced by black people living outside the main areas of settlement' which she feels are 'apparent from studies in Scotland, where the black community is relatively small'. She notes difficulties revealed by studies in Glasgow, and similarly in Sheffield (likewise with a relatively small black population), where 'no section of this community is unaffected by racist harassment'. Reporting a study by Sheffield City Council she observes that Chinese people had found the risk of violence 'almost as British as the weather' (Smith with Hill, 1991,p.22). Harassment may be linked with a variety of racisms or struggles about resources, and may manifest itself in fields other than housing (see for instance CRE, 1988b, which deals with education). In cases where such harassment is linked to housing, and relates to white pressure to keep black people out of an area, then one outcome may be a reluctance among minority ethnic households to stay in or move to good accommodation, and a retreat inside the home or to areas where black people are already numerous. Ginsburg - in a valuable review - argues that racial attacks, harassment and the threat of them are very significant in perpetuating 'second class welfare citizenship' for black people, and that the fear of possible anti-black racial violence is a factor that often motivates housing managers and black prospective tenants in allocating and choosing tenancies. He points out that 'racial violence and harassment in and around the home' are very important factors 'in sustaining racial inequalities in housing' (Ginsburg, 1989,p.66). As a Commission for Racial Equality report commented in the 1980s, there are 'many, effectively "no-go" areas which have acquired a "name" for racial harassment and where members of ethnic minorities are afraid to accept offers of homes, should they even be offered them' (1987,p.20). If defensive withdrawal strategies are adopted in the face of such violence, this can increase segregation.

Going beyond individual aggression, institutional complicity, and indirectly discriminatory practices, there are also direct infringements of the rights of black people by public agencies (see Smith, 1989,p.141), or denials that they have full rights. Hendessi refers, for example, to the 'widespread practice of passport checks, a form of internal immigration control, carried out by many London authorities', which has 'effectively excluded migrants from being considered for council housing' (1987,p.3; cf Henderson and Karn, 1987,pp.201-2). This type of approach apparently has been officially and legally endorsed recently.[5] One implication is that, by contrast with white households, black people may be expected to undergo more stringent tests and have their status questioned even when they are UK citizens. This may deter them from seeking certain housing solutions.

Segregation and citizenship

Before moving on to discuss housing material more directly, we need to comment explicitly on connections between racisms, segregation and citizenship. As our discussion has implied, segregation is a multi-faceted phenomenon, tightly linked with racism, harassment and discrimination, as well as with choices. Smith's work suggests that, in segregation, social and/or geographical differentiation is systematically organized and actively sustained through racist practices (see Smith, 1989, for discussion). It is important for us to keep in mind that segregation is not just a spatial process, but involves divisive or stratified structures of opportunity, rights and access. Smith shows how 'meaningful citizenship rights' - economic, social and political - are made less available to black people than to their white counterparts, and how these rights are 'manipulated through the practice of segregation to construct patterns of inequality' (p.8.). Geographical patterns of residential segregation may be seen to some extent as part of larger processes of exclusion, and this 'racial' segregation has been a 'consistent theme of this country's urban geography for more than forty years' (p.17). Although we must not overstate the spatial aspects, it is worth noting the possibility that once an association develops between particular localities and relative disadvantage, location can come to exert some 'independent' effect on both employment and housing opportunities for residents. Residence in a certain locality comes to be a factor effectively restricting access to good jobs, services and housing elsewhere, particularly at times of uneven growth and economic change affecting prosperity within areas. With relatively poor choices or capital assets in housing terms, little chance locally of top quality education or training, and a lack of job experience or investment capital, people may be trapped into remaining where they are in an economic as well as locality sense. Thus spatial segregation may be one 'medium for the reproduction of racial inequality' (Smith,p.105). Wrench et al. have also indicated that black migrants who go to more prosperous parts of the country may well come up against very direct racism, itself perhaps a deterrent to moving further afield (Wrench, Brar and Martin, 1993,pp.116-29). Our discussion of these issues, however, should not be taken to deny what we have already said earlier about the advantages of concentration and the important role played by the preferences of minority ethnic people. Rather, we are reasserting that there can be involuntary aspects of concentration linked to racist pressures and economic disadvantage, and that these might contribute (through maintaining segregation) to the reinforcement of general processes of exclusion.

Much of what we have been discussing so far can be cast in terms of differential citizenship (cf Ginsburg or Smith comments cited above). Minority ethnic households are likely to experience the law and order system and access to services differently from the majority of white households. Even the areas minorities live in may be subject to different policing practices or strategies from other areas; indeed some critics of the police might go so far as to claim an 'almost systematic disregard' for the civil liberties of black people (Institute of Race Relations, 1987,p.1,etc.). The status of members of ethnic minorities as citizens appears to be frequently inferior, and their opportunities for effective engagement or representation in politics may have been less than for white people.

The housing experience; conditions and general features

Although there is great diversity (which we comment on again below), in general terms the (non-white) minority ethnic population of Britain (numbering over three million) tends to be relatively poorly housed. This is despite the fact that the majority of groups have lived in the country for a long period of time, many black people having been born here. (A current estimate is that 46.8 per cent of all persons from minority ethnic groups were born in the UK, but this probably understates the true percentage: see Owen, 1993,p.12.) The 1991 census data provide information on aspects of physical housing deprivation, in terms of long-established conventional UK measures (see Owen, 1993a for figures). Publications are due to appear soon which will add to the detail available about the minorities.[6] Already, however, Owen has provided good basic housing information. Data on overcrowding, on lack of exclusive use of bath or WC, and on households not living in self-contained accommodation, all point towards relatively disadvantaged circumstances. For instance, the national figure for the percentage of all households affected by overcrowding is 2.2 per cent, but for minority ethnic households the figure is 13.1 per cent. In line with her analysis already referred to above, Smith has argued that the most striking element in the patterning of housing need among the UK's Asian and Afro-Caribbean populations is its localization. She states that residential segregation 'is an enduring feature of British urban life, at every spatial scale' (Smith with Hill, 1991,p.18). In broad terms the 1991 census bears this out, confirming the marked geographical concentration of the ethnic minorities within parts of England. There are many places where specific ethnic groups are concentrated, often in poor quality housing; examples are covered in studies like Eade's work on Bangladeshis in East London (1989), or Habeebullah and Slater's study in Rochdale (1990). There are also many predominantly 'white areas' of severe deprivation, but as already discussed black communities suffer extra difficulties arising from racism and a history of neglect by housing agencies. Census data on settlement patterns show that the highest relative concentrations of people from ethnic minorities are found in London, and that ethnic minorities are least well represented in the higher status growth areas and the more rural parts of Britain. There is apparently a tendency for the growing ethnic minority population to be increasingly spatially concentrated, in the larger urban settlements of Britain (for figures and commentary see Owen, 1992).

Some general national statistics on the role of public sector housing agencies in meeting minority ethnic needs are available, although there are limits in the degree of detail; for example, agencies have not necessarily measured the relative quality of rented units allocated to households from different ethnic categories. At the time of the most recent census, local authorities housed 21.4 per cent of all British households, including 21.8 per cent of the minority ethnic households, while housing associations catered for 3.1 per cent of households, including 5.9 per cent of the ethnic minority ones (Owen, 1993a). Despite central government policies to reduce the importance of council housing, British local authorities and similar bodies still manage around five million dwellings (Central Statistical Office, 1993,p.113), but local authorities have been losing units while the associations taken as a whole have been growing. This means that much of the best new social rented stock is now being built by housing associations, and makes their activities very significant for prospective tenants from ethnic minorities in some localities. Since 1981 the number of households renting from housing associations has increased by 70 per cent while the number renting from local authorities has decreased by 11 per cent (Champion and Dorling, 1993). Both the housing associations and local authorities house a greater proportion of pensioner households, lone parents, and households headed by women than are found in the population as a whole. Housing associations, however - as can be deduced from figures above - seem to have a higher proportion of minority ethnic households among their tenants than do local authorities; the figure appears highest for London, where 20.8 per cent of association tenant households are recorded as being from ethnic minorities (Champion and Dorling, 1993).

It is important to add some observations on the diversity of experiences and preferences. Both for localities and for ethnic groups there can be significant variations in tenure and conditions, and this has been recognized in studies over the years. Rich refers to 'the dimension of ethnic exclusivity which makes home

67

ownership a vital component of Asian communal identity' (1987,p.77), and this type of view conjours up a stereotype of the Asian person as a would-be owner-occupier. Although this may be based on a reality in broad terms, purchasers have not always had any alternative way of getting access to cheap or decent homes (McKay, 1977,pp.83-4). Furthermore, different communities may experience differing economic circumstances and may have divergent preferences and options. Consequently outcomes vary. In the 1980s Brown noted differences, for instance, in levels of owner-occupation between Asian groups; at the time of the third Policy Studies Institute survey (in 1982) only 30 per cent among Bangladeshis, yet 91 per cent amongst Sikhs (Brown, 1984,p.69). Among West Indians at that time there were more council tenants than owners (p.68). Brown suggested that tenure patterns were 'tending to become even more ethnically polarised...'(p.69).

Recent census data indicate continuing diversities in tenure and in household characteristics and formation. Although more material is likely to be published later, excellent summary analyses have already been provided from the National Ethnic Minority Data Archive at Warwick (see Owen, 1993a). For present purposes we can draw on these for illustrations of diversity. For example, Owen comments on the comparatively large average size of South Asian households, with Pakistani households containing just under five people on average, while 'Bangladeshi households are more than twice as large as the overall national average'. There appear to be relatively few single-adult households in this group, but the proportion of households containing three or more adults is high. By contrast, although the average number of people in Black households (here meaning African, Caribbean, etc.) is slightly higher than the overall average, approaching a half of all Black households contain only one adult (Owen, 1993a,p.2). Major differences appear between minority ethnic groups in the proportion of households owning or buying their homes. The overall figures indicate only two fifths of Black households (as defined in this census analysis), compared to nearly four fifths of South Asian households, and more than half of the 'Chinese and other' non-white households census category (Owen, 1993a,p.7). Within these broad categories there are again significant differences. For instance, while 48.1 per cent of Black Caribbean households are home-owners, only 28.0 per cent of Black African households are. Similarly, within the South Asian category, 81.7 per cent of Indian households are home-owners, but only 44.5 per cent of Bangladeshis (p.7; cf Brown's figures above). The individual ethnic groups 'most dependent upon the public sector for housing' are 'Black-Africans and Bangladeshis', but even for these groups 'it only provides accommodation for two-fifths of all households' (Owen, 1993a,p.8). More than a tenth of ethnic minority households rent from a private landlord, 'with nearly a fifth of Chinese and others in this tenure category' (this compares with only 7.1 per cent of households overall in privately rented dwellings) (p.8).

The complexities of circumstances revealed by this type of information and by earlier work imply caution in public policies. Stereotypes - such as the idea that one group or other particularly favours or disregards owner-occupation, or that some communities will always look after their older people - need to be viewed with considerable circumspection. Patel has noted, for instance, the 'erroneous assumption that the extended family system will cater for all, including the elderly...' (1987,p.90). As far as owner-occupation is concerned, however, that is clearly a topic of importance to many groups. It should not be forgotten, furthermore, that although the majority of minority ethnic owner-occupiers are still concentrated in older, lower status neighbourhoods, there is movement into higher status property outside 'deprived areas', albeit 'characterised by new nodes of ethnic minority concentration' (Phillips and Karn, 1992,p.358).

The research record

Having outlined the overall picture, we now need to comment directly on specific research. This account will not highlight important contributions to theory which have been made in conjunction with 'race' and housing material, as in the very well known Rex and Moore study (1967), or in Rex and Tomlinson (1979), Sarre, Phillips and Skellington (1989), or Smith (1989). Although the present chapter has been influenced by the above writers there is no intention to give a history of theories here. Instead we shall refer to empirical findings, and emphasize recent research trends.

The record of UK investigations into housing conditions and institutional practices affecting ethnic minorities is stunningly good, despite gaps in coverage. This strong record has come about partly because of a continuing official agency concern to discover the extent of discriminatory activities, to understand their nature, and to combat them. In particular the *Commission for Racial Equality* (CRE) has produced or commissioned a large number of revealing studies with this kind of focus over a number of years, an achievement of which the agency can be justly proud. Some have been formal investigations aimed at finding whether discrimination has occurred in order to take corrective action; others have been less legally driven. Amongst matters dealt with have been the behaviour of private sector housing organizations, exchange professionals and intermediaries, including building societies, estate agents, landlords, etc., the practices of local authorities, and the performance of housing associations.[7] In addition the CRE has published guidance on good practice,[8] and advice on how to achieve equality even in relatively under-researched areas (such as co-ops; see 1991).

The 'race' and housing field has also attracted efforts by independent researchers based in housing agency, academic or pressure group settings. They too have worked on several fronts. There have been many excellent analyses in the field of *local authority housing*.[9] There has also been some work on *housing association activity* (see Niner, 1984 and 1987).[10] Much of the research on local authorities has revealed discriminatory practices and outcomes, particularly in council house allocation. The material complements CRE work already noted above, such as the investigation of race and council housing in Hackney (1984). Housing officers may feel a 'need' to fill properties in less desirable areas as quickly as possible, and may offer such dwellings to urgent cases with little choice, often including black households. Lacking knowledge of estates and facilities, and facing the twin pressures of urgency and hostility, black people find their 'negotiating power' with housing departments cut away (cf CRE, 1984b,p.40). White households more willing or able to wait - or already in council housing and awaiting a transfer - can eventually go to better estates. Put more negatively, white people may battle to keep black people out of preferred areas, referring to the merits of ideas of queuing which disadvantage newcomers, and citing the need to earn each move up a ladder of housing desirability through time and acceptable behaviour (see Eade, 1989,pp.130-40). Such grass roots attitudes may be reflected within agencies. Black people may be disadvantaged by unfavourable stereotyping applied to them by officers, whereby households are assumed to have certain characteristics which make it appropriate to 'match them up' with specific inferior types of properties. Ethnic minorities may face difficulties because of language barriers, may be intimidated (by local white people) when viewing accommodation, and may be at a disadvantage in choosing locations because of limitations in the supply of stock appropriate to their needs or preferences. Some local authorities may have concentrated building or renovation programmes on types of dwellings which will not meet the needs of large households from black communities, while substantial urban renewal programmes may not have benefited black households greatly.

Writers have also discussed the behaviour of *private sector agencies* and the experiences of black households in *owner-occupation* or *private renting*.[11] Over the years evidence has appeared about difficuties in obtaining mortgages, about exclusionary practices by white landlords, about dual markets for housing in which black people might be served separately or at higher costs, on 'steering' of minority ethnic purchasers towards particular parts of the market by estate agents, and a variety of other problems. For private renting, accommodation agencies may have discriminated - alongside individual landlords - against black people (CRE, 1990). It is important to add two points to the general picture of public and private sector experiences. First, research indicates a wide variety of circumstances and practices, albeit with consistency amongst them. Second, minority ethnic people are not necessarily passive participants. They have followed various paths to try to improve their positions. In a sophisticated summary of past and present situations for owner-occupation, Phillips and Karn observe that there has been a 'close and dynamic relationship between individual strategies, institutional behaviour and the wider social, economic and political structure', as housing purchasers and institutions have responded to each other 'within a framework of local and national change'. The route of minority ethnic purchasers into owner-occupation has often been 'unconventional and costly', with first-time buyers being 'deprived of any significant choice in either housing type or location' (Phillips and Karn, 1992,p.358). Even so, the authors indicate that private housing market institutions are far from monolithic in their responses to minority ethnic clients, and that there is evidence that moves up-market into the suburbs by more affluent members of the ethnic minorities have become more extensive over time, even if within limited geographical areas (pp.359,363-4).

Despite variations, however, there is continuing evidence appearing of adverse experiences for many people from black communities. Housing market disadvantage, generated by low economic status of households, has been reinforced by discriminatory institutional and individual behaviour amongst 'gatekeepers' who influence access to dwellings or funds. The twin problems faced by most (although not all) minority ethnic households - lack of financial resources and lack of political leverage - largely account for their relatively poor dwelling conditions. In addition, black people experience harassment or may be forced to take avoidance strategies because of an anticipation of discrimination or hostility, and are disproportionately vulnerable to homelessness (see Black Housing, 1989).[12] Furthermore, through the overall pattern of experiences of varied groups runs the factor of *enforced dependence*. Even though minority ethnic households have participated heavily in house purchase and improvement, and have become clients of public agencies, the housing institutions have on the whole remained white run. Sarre, Phillips and Skellington note that for Bedford, the minorities have dealt with mainstream institutions rather than develop their own housing businesses, and remain largely in the hands of white policy makers (1989,p.298; but cf Cater, 1981). This kind of pattern may have been changing (slowly), and there are many exceptions, but the statement highlights the fact that others have profited greatly from the presence of black people in the housing market, while the share of gains to black run businesses and employees may have been small in relative terms. Where minority ethnic entrepreneurs have gained a share of housing business - as in the case of landlords - this may have been in a context of dual market conditions.

Although adverse patterns of minority ethnic housing experience are intimately connected with racism, it is worth remembering that *racism itself operates alongside or in conjunction with other 'discourses' or ideologies* that differentiate the so-called respectables and less respectables in housing.[13] Groups seen as less deserving - which frequently have included black households but also can include lesbians, gays, single parents, disabled people and so forth - are open to exclusion and stigmatization in many areas of daily life. Such processes of social division may have pre-dated the arrival of black people in large numbers in Britain and pre-date the apparatus of the modern welfare state. In present day western societies, however, they are overlaid, amplified or mediated by behavioural features of bureaucratic allocation systems and by market characteristics such as risk avoidance by lenders. Interestingly, the assessment of relative risk might enter into evaluations in private and public housing sectors. Just as the building society manager in the 1970s weighed up a potential borrower (or the valuer weighed up the property and its locality) with a view to the security of the society's investment, so the council housing manager could weigh up the tenant with a view to 'protecting' the best estates and dwellings. Historically, this tended to take on spatial dimensions (for the mortgages example see Harrison and Stevens, 1982), with segregation and risk evaluation not reflecting racism alone, but a variety of other factors too. On the other hand there have been instances where local authority practices have appeared to complement or compensate for private market systems. For instance, mortgage lending by councils - although subject to some of the usual risk evaluation criteria - may have been of considerable help to minorities if they found access to building society loans more problematic.[14]

Gaps and developments in research

Reviewing the overall research record on 'race' and housing, one can see that certain sectors have been covered more fully than others. Lack of data or problems of access create obstacles in researching private sector activity. Consequently, as Smith puts it in a report for the Joseph Rowntree Foundation,

> In contrast to the body of work accumulating on the problems of discrimination in the...public sectors, work on the privately rented and owner occupied sectors, with only a few exceptions, is generally either dated, very small in scale, over-speculative or simply non-existent. (Smith with Hill, 1991,p.65).

Even here, however, there is enough evidence to suggest continued patterns of disadvantage. Some groups - such as certain newer migrants - clearly suffer severe hardships.[15] For owner-occupiers there are continuing constraints on choice produced by the attitudes of the white population and white professionals (Phillips and Karn, 1992,p.367). It would be useful to have more research on low cost owner-occupation, and particularly on the extent to which black people have benefited from governmental programmes (shared ownership, etc.). Another gap in research information concerns the 'life-course' experience within ethnic groups; a perspective here is needed to indicate how disadvantages resulting from discrimination experienced at one point in the housing career accumulate or are reduced by subsequent changes (see Smith with Hill, 1991,p.66). Again, we need to remember the importance of strategies pursued by minority ethnic households themselves.

Efforts continue to extend knowledge. Recent research studies have included coverage of council house sales and African/Caribbean tenants (Peach and Byron, 1994), housing and refugees (JRF, 1993), comparative public housing segregation in England and the USA (Goering, 1993), ethnic elders (FBHO, 1990; Shah and Williams, 1992), and the impact of housing investment decision making (Mullings, 1991). Exploring the relatively neglected topic of local authority investment, Mullings writes that the 'difficulties involved in the successful programming of large scale renovation and repair on the majority of difficult-to-let estates', produce discriminatory effects 'on the large numbers of black households disproportionately represented on these estates' (1991,p.43). This research parallels or revives an interest of writers about earlier periods who commented on slum clearance, urban improvement, and renewal processes and their impact (see for example Jacobs, 1985,pp.19-21; McKay, 1977,pp.91-2; and Duke, 1970). Clearly it is desirable to consider local investment and renewal and regulatory processes affecting the stock, alongside allocation patterns. Equally important is the need to monitor how central governmental strategies for subsidies and incentives may privilege or close down routes accessible to one group more than another (this fits with our perspective in chapter 2). Co-op housing, housing association provision, local authority provision, and private sector opportunities are all influenced by central government plans and funding, with many differential effects.[16] Turning to a different concern, our recent work on contractors described in chapter 6 of this book has broken new ground. It reveals that if one looks at the indirect beneficiaries of social housing investment there is little evidence of black communities taking a substantial share through building or services contracts. This extends what is known about the proportion of the business and employment benefits of housing activity going to minority ethnic communities. Another important step forward is the CRE's recent investigation of housing associations, which has shown association practices still to be deficient in several respects, and has raised some particular questions about the state of housing practice in Scotland (1993). Sometimes a realization of past deficiencies in practice has led to a more sensitive response from providers; for

73

example, the need for cultural sensitivity in design and planning is now more acknowledged than in the past (see Penoyre and Prasad et al., 1993). Similarly, private housing market intermediaries may nowadays be more interested in generating ethnic minority custom, and 'a few institutions have specifically modified their practices to accommodate the cultural norms of minority clients' (Phillips and Karn, 1992,p.361).

It is likely that an increasing amount of material will become available over the next few years on areas of specialized provision and needs, including work on the housing/medical/social care boundaries, where there has already been considerable interest (as with Jones, 1994, on sheltered accommodation; or Baylies, Law and Mercer, 1993, on support after discharge from psychiatric hospitals). It is to be hoped that there will also be much more work on housing needs and experiences for minority ethnic women,[17] and for disabled people among minority ethnic communities (as in Begum, 1992,4.6). We agree with Smith, who says that the literature indicates that there are distinctive clusters of unmet need, arising from the ethnocentrism of the housing system, which interact with institutionalized racism to produce a range of groups whose housing needs require further investigation (Smith with Hill, 1991,pp.29-30). This requirement for investigation may be heightened where there is an additional issue of gender, disability or health.

Prospects for co-operation in research

One problem for investigations has been the difficulty of ensuring full awareness of minority ethnic perspectives on research areas and priorities. It has not been easy for established researchers to keep in touch with such perspectives. Apart from the many studies written up in books and journals, however - and publications by organizations such as the London Race and Housing Research Unit - there are local needs projects, critical enquiries, and other types of work which may be reported in charity or practitioner publications, less formally, or in documents that are given a narrower circulation. Some of these investigations have been initiated by minority ethnic organizations or individuals, or in partnerships which involve them.[18] Furthermore, although black people have not been well represented among established housing research staff and scholars in mainstream university departments, their input here has been growing through involvements via local housing agencies and through co-operative ventures with universities. For example, at time of writing the Universities of Leeds, Manchester, and York each have research projects in hand in conjunction with partners or consultants from black run housing organizations. The 'Race' and Public Policy (RAPP) research unit at Leeds has a Nuffield Foundation project on young black homeless people run jointly with CHAR and the Federation of

Black Housing Organisations (FBHO), and is hosting a study on needs and options led from a group of organizations including Unity (one of the North's leading minority ethnic housing associations). RAPP has also just completed a project on housing contractors (referred to above) for which the London Equal Opportunities Federation acted in a consultancy capacity. York University is involved with work alongside Sadeh Lok, another important Yorkshire black led housing association, while Manchester University is carrying out a study on minority ethnic housing associations with the FBHO as consultant. This trend is likely to help make research projects more sensitive to community concerns, experience and understanding, and to some extent is matched in other fields outside housing.

Minority ethnic organizations, politics and strategies

It can be argued that the UK political system has operated as much to control and contain political struggles from black communities as to accommodate them. Bulpitt's analysis suggests that 'race politics' has been managed in order to satisfy the interests of elites at the centre of politics, with the interests of 'blacks and whites in the periphery' being 'left to chance'. He also observes that 'blacks were faced with a fundamentally unhelpful local political structure, highly resistant to their political demands' (1986,pp.23 and 34). At this level minority ethnic organizations may have experienced marginalisation, with anti-racist forces being pushed 'away from the centre, towards the periphery of local politics' (Ben-Tovim, Gabriel, Law and Stredder, 1986,p.135). Thus racialized minorities may have had limited scope for productive participation in mainstream representative politics.

Although they have made gains, ethnic minorities have been under-represented in local authorities as councillors; at national level they have fared even worse.[19] Even when elected, the capacity of some black representatives to pursue the interests of their communities may have been inhibited by the requirements of participating in a party sytem in which white people's votes remain crucial. This could constrain their actions within either party, but there is also the difficulty that the party which attracts them less has held power centrally for a very long period. Those locally-developed strategies which have been tried - as with multi-culturalism or anti-racism - could fall foul of hostility from a Conservative Party keen to discipline councils run by its opponents. Indeed some strategies to accommodate black people's needs and preferences can be portrayed as a threat to 'British traditions'. In addition, a racialized discourse around culture may have undermined political struggles within Asian communities for representation (Solomos and Back, 1994,157). Nonetheless, despite obstacles, communities have been exerting influence, and in places black political representation is already 'secure and will constitute a significant force' (Solomos and Back, 1991,p.35), even if political impact as yet remains greater at local than national level. Insofar as local authorities still exert power - directly or indirectly - over housing provision, increased influence of black people is likely to help minority ethnic households with their accommodation.

Conventional party politics does not exhaust the possibilities of political participation or collective action. Ramdin gives a solid account of the history of struggles, noting that wherever and whenever 'exploitation had become unbearable', black people fought for redress, 'particularly at the workplace' (1987,p.508). Outside industrial relations (although not always unconnected with employment) there are several non-electoral means for voicing concerns or putting on pressure. At one end of the spectrum of possibilities is the street disturbance, violent protest, riot, or uprising (the preferred term varying according to political standpoint).[20] This may be partly interpreted as an attempt to express the frustrations of political exclusion, articulated through conflict with the police in particular. Then there are other forms of direct action such as self-defence groups, which may also be a means of bringing about alterations in official agency practices (e.g. on tenancies or harassment). Mobilizations may also arise around specific services and provisions, either along mixed membership lines or through groups formed exclusively around the concept of their black identity, their religious allegiance, etc. Aims may vary, including self help and social care objectives as well as 'pressure group' activity. Within white run organizations there may be trends for establishing separate committees, networks or sections for black people, although not necessarily free of constraints (see for instance Shukra, 1990; Jeffers, 1991 and 1993).

Turning to housing, we can see that much more research material has been gathered on conditions and discrimination against consumers than directly on housing action from within minority communities, although Eade's study is a notable exception (1989, chapter 5). The internal politics and staffing of agencies from a 'race' perspective also remains an under-researched issue.[21] The emphasis has begun to change, however, as activists and scholars have recognized the importance of charting histories and taking more account of achievements by minority ethnic groups. The black voluntary housing movement and minority ethnic housing associations have been attracting particular attention recently, perhaps partly because of their relative success in breaking into the world of financial resources and institutional influence (albeit despite obstacles). Their development has also helped bring to prominence concerns about cultural sensitivity related to such areas as design.[22] In any event, their significance is widely recognized;[23] the Manchester University research referred to above will provide the first systematic comparative material on black and white run housing associations.

Growing recognition of black people's contributions to housing knowledge and change is part of a wider acknowledgement of the need to study political and organizational contributions, issues of leadership, and participation (see for instance contributions in Werbner and Anwar, 1991). It is accepted that minority ethnic communities cannot be studied merely as recipients of policies which disadvantage them, but are actively engaged in negotiation, pressure, and struggles for improvement. The communities, their construction, and their experiences may be complex as far as representation, internal politics, goals and interests are concerned (see Eade, 1989 and 1991).

At the micro-level some scattered information emerged on organizational development over the last decade as a by-product of studying the operations of the Urban Programme; particularly material on the voluntary sector and the obstacles small black run organizations faced. The phrase 'funding for failure' sometimes seemed appropriate, signifying official support but not enough to avoid a precarious existence or even eventual collapse; and it was evident that dependency on larger white run organizations and council departments could be a key issue. Although varied objectives were evident in the voluntary sector bids for Urban Programme funding up to the early 1980s, general needs housing action was perhaps not a central strand for black led bodies at this time. On the other hand, some black housing practitioners may have 'cut their teeth' during these years on work in the area of specialized needs provision (such as via hostels or refuges). The period running up to the early 1980s is important, but unfortunately data are scarce. Julienne has commented that the history of the development of black and minority ethnic housing organizations, 'including specialist ones like refuges and hostels,' has still to be written (Foreword to Harrison, 1991). From the mid 1980s we have more accessible housing action information, not least because of the availability of the journal Black Housing. One possibility about the earlier years is that - despite the frustrations of marginalisation and tokenism in resource terms - the Urban Programme and other locally orientated initiatives did provide a stimulus or invitation to particular organizational forms, and in that sense sometimes offered terrain on which interests could coalesce, mobilize and move forward. This is a view that can be put forward more definitely in relation to the later period and the Housing Corporation's programme for minority ethnic housing associations, which will be covered in the next chapter. At the same time we can see that in the context of local government's urban policies activists could become familiar with a variety of practical strategies they might pursue. Working within and outside white run organizations, they could target both improvement of practices within existing agencies, and creation of new and more representative organizations for their communities. Here the word empowerment could be very appropriate. Faced with difficulties in 'bending' mainstream services and organizations in culturally sensitive or anti-racist directions, housing practitioners from minority ethnic communities might consider 'separatist' approaches. The argument would be that although improved practices within 'mainstream' housing organizations bring benefits (Harrison, 1992), this must be supplemented by independent organizational development. Only then would minority ethnic voices have adequate access to policy making settings, and only through their own organizations would black people achieve fair chances in terms of careers or consumer influence on provision. This set of themes underpins the struggle to establish and sustain the minority ethnic organizations which are the main subject for our next chapter. The facts of segregation also contribute, since a concentration of people with similarly severe problems, and (sometimes) a great deal in common, can encourage locality based attempts to address housing need, giving motivation to black led housing organizations. None of this is meant to deny the possibilities of tokenism, defusing of protest, and potential divisiveness of some official programmes, or the danger of being 'sucked into competing' for grants in a process which can necessitate 'accommodation and conformity with certain norms' (Lloyd, 1994,p.230).

Having focussed on community action - and thereby set the scene for our next chapter - we should note that the *collective routes* we are discussing *are always operating alongside* other *more individualized strategies*. Households and small groupings based around cultural, business and kinship links may pursue housing advance through a variety of means, of which owner-occupation is one. Collective action could facilitate or help sustain owner-occupancy, so there is no clear divide between forms of available action and tenure categories. (Nor is there always a clear divide between employment possibilities, accommodation, social care, and investment.) Nonetheless, it is as well to remember that the diversity of housing outcomes observed in studies may fit to some extent with a diversity of strategies and options. Certainly, the research and data records show how very significant ownership has been, even though household tenure choices have been constrained by racism and economic circumstances. Any discussion of the collective empowerment of communities needs to bear this in mind. At the same time we need to remember the salience of individualized rights and systems of choice when we consider collective representation and action in the later parts of our book. In this way we will be following the line marked out in earlier chapters, which presented welfare systems and empowerment as embracing very wide ranges of activity.

A summary of key conclusions

This chapter has covered a great deal of ground, even though we have had to be selective in choosing which published studies to refer to. It may be helpful to summarize the main points:-

(a) Through a combination of economic disadvantage, racist discrimination, and political exclusion, non-white minority ethnic groups have tended to suffer inferior housing conditions. Although minority ethnic communities vary in the precise nature of their housing experiences, there are clear patterns. We can treat these as outcomes of processes of welfare state differentiation and representation which were considered in chapter 2. In this context we are likely to find that racist practices operate alongside other discourses and actions which disadvantage 'less respectable' categories of consumers. We can also see adverse housing treatment as an aspect of the differentiation of citizenship itself.

(b) Concentration in particular localities may reflect preferences and perceived advantages as well as constraints, but may itself also reduce opportunities for residents in some ways. The crucial factor is the amount of real choice which residents feel they have.

(c) Although the options open to black and minority ethnic households have been restricted, groups and individuals nonetheless have pursued a variety of strategies to try to improve their housing circumstances. Paths chosen have ranged from seeking individual owner-occupation to embarking on collective actions in the political forum. Although we tend to think in terms of specifically housing strategies, it is worth remembering that households or wider groupings may not necessarily treat accommodation needs in isolation from other aspects of life; including investment, work, businesses, and social care. Individual and collective actions may reflect this. To some extent the prospects and forms of action can also be shaped by the specific commercial, political and institutional environments which households face.

(d) Much of the best research has focussed on the disadvantaged treatment of households as consumers, and the conflicts that situations of rationing, shortage or investment prioritizing tend to heighten. There is also good material beginning to appear on gender, problems of special needs groups, etc. More neglected, however, have been the 'indirect' aspects of the housing experience, in terms of the benefits that flow to producers, exchange professionals and other intermediaries. In a sense our work on contractors in chapter 6 offers an initial insight into part of that terrain.

Notes

1. For fuller comment, and reservations about notions of communities, see chapter 1, which also contains a statement on use of the terms 'black' and 'minority ethnic'.
2. For discussions of dispersal issues see Flett, 1984 and 1984a; Smith, 1977, chapter 13; Henderson and Karn, 1987, chapter 9; McKay, 1977, chapter 6.
3. The strength of one community in an area need not make life politically comfortable for groups that are less numerous there; see for instance Jeffers, 1993,p.167.
4. See The Guardian, 3 December 1994. For a summary of some information on relevant topics see Home Office, 1994,pp.12-16.
5. See reports on recent legal case and ministerial reaction, The Guardian, 16 April 1993 and 26 May 1993.
6. See forthcoming work by a large group of scholars, to be published in several volumes by OPCS, 1995. (Editors are Coleman, D. and Salt, J.; Ratcliffe, P.; Karn, V.; Peach, C.).
7. For instance see CRE, 1982, 1983, 1984, 1984a, 1984b, 1985, 1988, 1988a, 1990, 1990a, 1993, London Race and Housing Forum, 1981, Dalton and Daghlian, 1989.
8. For example a code of practice in rented housing; CRE, 1991a.
9. For example see material in Rex and Tomlinson, 1979; Henderson and Karn, 1987; Phillips, 1986; Sarre, Phillips and Skellington, 1989, chapter 6; Simpson, 1981; Ginsburg, 1988/89 and1989; Burney, 1967; Smith, 1977, chapter 11; Habeebullah and Slater, 1990.
10. See also Simpson, 1981,p.237, for comments on the impact of the local authority/housing association relationship.
11. For instance see Karn, Kemeny and Williams, 1985; Smith, 1977, chapter 12; Brown, 1984,pp.78-80; Sarre, Phillips and Skellington, 1989, chapter 7; Fenton and Collard, 1984; Doling and Davies, 1983; Hendessi, 1987, chapter 2; Harrison and Stevens, 1981. For a review of the private rented scene see Smith, 1989,pp.81-4, and for a convenient summary of some of the earlier private sector studies see McKay, 1977, chapter 4.
12. For an interesting example of a relevant study on minority ethnic homelessness see Ye-Myint, 1992.
13. For relevant comments see Henderson and Karn, 1984; Phillips, 1986,pp.33-4; Jacobs, 1985,pp.22-3; Burney 1967,p.76.
14. See comments in Niner, 1975,pp.76-80; Burney, 1967,p.34; Rex and Tomlinson, 1979,pp.129,146-7; although see also Sarre, Phillips and Skellington, 1989,p.275. See also Harrison and Stevens, 1981.
15. See Hendessi, 1987,pp.8-12, 28-31, including comments on tied housing.

16. See for instance Solomos, 1991,pp.155-6, on the relevance of local authority resource constraints, etc.
17. See the review in Smith with Hill, 1991,pp.30-1; and Dhillon-Kashyap, 1994, who includes comment on Rao, 1990, and Mama, 1989.
18. A good example is Hajimichael, 1988. A project currently in hand is a study to investigate the housing needs and aspirations of black people in *Calderdale*, which began in August 1994 and is supervized by a steering group including a representative of Nashayman housing association. In the *West Midlands* there is a study related to elders, commissioned by Nehemiah from Dixon and Turkington at the University of Central England; see Housing Associations Weekly, 9 September 1994, 378,p.13.
19. For a range of interesting material on politics see Goulbourne, 1990.
20. For a summary of comments on disturbances see Smith, 1989,pp.163-7.
21. Although see Hajimichael, 1988, including housing associations staffing; the NFHA and CRE have also surveyed aspects of internal association practice. In addition see Lush and Beeby, 1993, and FBHO, 1994.
22. For some issues see Penoyre and Prasad et al., 1993, and Harrison, 1992a.
23. The present writer knows of two postgraduate theses and several undergraduate dissertations completed or in hand on black run associations, and there are likely to be others.

5 'Social housing' and the Black Voluntary Housing Movement

Having sketched the broad record and findings of UK 'race' and housing research, we now turn to a specific area of investigation within that field. This chapter and the next one focus on aspects of 'social rented housing', where housing associations have been playing increasingly important roles as developers and providers of dwellings. The conclusions to chapter 4 included the observation that groups and individuals have pursued a variety of strategies to try to improve their housing circumstances. One of the routes used has been through the creation of independent housing organizations run by minority ethnic people themselves. This is the subject of the present chapter.[1]

The achievements of the black voluntary housing movement in Britain are probably still relatively unknown outside the UK. Yet experiences here in the 1980s and early 1990s may be of considerable interest for an international audience aware of the needs, pressures and difficulties of ethnic pluralism. There may be comparisons to make in the future, lessons to be drawn about community empowerment, and insights that may help inform the development of theory. In the sections below we summarize some key events and issues, emphasizing the unusual character of public policies pursued by the English Housing Corporation, and noting the high profile of the black voluntary housing movement. Unlike many accounts of public policy and 'race', this is not a story of failure. Far from it. Despite continuing obstacles and an uncertain future there has been a considerable degree of success. The discussion below will describe how in the 1980s and early 1990s the black voluntary housing movement helped bring about (and subsequently continued to influence) one of the most significant developments across the whole range of UK social policies.

The rest of this chapter is in five parts. It begins with an introduction to the way that so-called social housing is organized and provided in Britain. Most UK readers will find this familiar territory. In the second section we comment on the research basis and data limitations of our material. The third part of the chapter then describes the English Housing Corporation's strategy and some of the results. We follow this up by considering the place of the black voluntary housing movement in the events of the 1980s, aspects of the movement's relationships with public policy, and issues of incorporation, cohesion and solidarity. Finally the chapter concludes with an overview on empowerment. We will consider the achievement of practical forms of empowerment, noting the property dimension as well as the vulnerability of resource provision that is selective rather than universalistic.

An introduction to the social housing scene

Although the major UK participant in providing subsidised rented housing has been local government, housing associations also play a role (see Cope, 1990, for an introduction). In the 1980s this increased as central government sought to diminish local authority functions, and perceived in the housing association movement an opportune substitute.

There has been a long tradition of central governments giving support to and helping to plan and guide local authority housing activity, stretching back to the years after World War One. This has primarily meant subsidising and supervising the construction and renting of council owned housing. The terms 'social housing' or 'social rented housing' have come into wide use in the UK relatively recently to denote dwellings owned by a recognised agency which rents accommodation to tenants in need. These institutional landlords include housing associations alongside local authorities. Central government has frequently offered 'bricks and mortar' subsidy, which has helped keep down the amount of costs carried by rents, both for council housing and housing association tenants. Since 1979 ministers have shifted the emphasis of subsidy away from bricks and mortar and towards selective means tested support, with rent levels rising as a consequence. The dominant suppliers in this sphere have remained local authorities, but from the end of the 1970s Conservative governments mounted a powerful attack on the council house tradition, encouraging sales to sitting tenants and - as the 1980s went on - transfers of entire estates to other landlords.[2] The transfer of estates with households still in them has proved a slower policy to implement than sales to tenants, and so far the easiest way to achieve it has been to use existing or newly established housing associations as the appropriate vehicles. At the same time new social housing investment has been directed to housing associations in preference to local authorities. Thus UK housing associations now have much more importance than they did prior to the mid-1980s (see Randolph, 1993, for trends in investment, etc.). This has not found favour with all anti-collectivist writers, since it appears to elevate housing associations at the potential expense of supporting more market orientated landlords (see Coleman, 1991, and reply, Murie, 1991). Perhaps, however, there are political and economic complications which until recently inhibited the development of more direct support for private landlords and profit making development companies; the housing associations themselves have considerable potential for lobbying and pressure, social housing tenants on means tested benefits are generally seen as an unreliable focus for private investment (unless investors are heavily shielded from risk of loss), and tenants' organizations and local authorities may themselves resist attempts at full privatization. A cynic might suggest that the easiest line for the government to have gone down in the late 1980s was a route via housing associations, which often have a relatively benign image, and that as with other programmes of privatization this may open up prospects for moves towards fuller and more ruthless recommodification in the future if the Conservative Party retains office. One idea fashionable at the level of discussion at present is to create special 'housing companies' to take over from local authorities (or associations), but the impact of such a move would depend very much on the financial and legal details.

On the other hand, at present there is still a great deal of continuity, and considerable similarity between the established functions of local authorities and those developing for housing associations. Indeed, many links exist between the two. Housing associations house substantial numbers of people in need nominated to them by councils, and like local authorities many have had to deal with increasing numbers of homeless (see JRF, 1994e). There is also some evidence that the kinds of problems experienced on local authority estates may be appearing in large housing association estates too (JRF, 1993a), although this is disputed.

The housing associations

British housing associations can vary greatly in constitution and management, and in the types of provision in which they engage. The more important associations, however, primarily provide housing for rent. By the early 1990s over 700,000 rented units were owned by housing associations in England, far fewer than owned by local authorities, but very much a growing sector.[3] Many housing associations are charitable in constitutional and legal terms, and managed by committees of a voluntary character, although employing professional staff. They tend to be referred to by the umbrella term the 'voluntary housing movement', which distinguishes them from local authorities and private landlords. This is not strictly logical, since local authorities are run by councillors, who serve voluntarily as unpaid committee members! The associations, however, are seen as being to a degree independent of party

84

politics, unlike councils, and there is a long established UK custom of referring to a wide range of non elected non profit agencies as 'voluntary' bodies. (We follow that practice in this book.)

The interests of housing associations are represented by national level organizations, the most important for our study being the National Federation of Housing Associations (NFHA) and the Federation of Black Housing Organisations (FBHO). The NFHA operates in England and has about 2,000 member associations, although not all are very active in housing development. It campaigns on their behalf, offers guidance on good practice, and is consulted by government. The FBHO represents a range of minority ethnic organizations connected with housing, including black run housing associations. An organization can be a member of the FBHO as well as the NFHA. Although smaller in staff and resources terms than the NFHA, the FBHO has also participated through consultations with government and the Housing Corporation (for instance see Black Housing, October/November 1989,p.22; FBHO Annual Report 1993/94,p.5).

Most of the substantial public funds channelled to associations in recent years have come through non elected bodies; bureaucratic ones established by central government.[4] In England the agency which distributes funds in this way is the Housing Corporation. Apart from offering the larger part of the available funding, and deciding its distribution, it exercises certain supervisory and administrative functions, thereby acting as a regulator of what is in many respects still a relatively independent movement. Only associations which the Corporation is prepared to formally register can hope to secure housing association grant (for which they can bid periodically). An association which is not yet registered may be supported indirectly, for example by benefiting from working with a registered association which has control of a capital allocation. Small or new associations may work with larger and more established partners in this way, although unless subsequently registered the small organization will never fully control the assets (or be likely to own the dwellings built).

Housing associations have a long history and have been diverse. While some have been supported by generous funds and have become major charities or businesses, others have been small and precarious. Although our account below is mainly about the last decade, there were a few attempts to establish associations to serve the needs of black people in earlier periods. Some records encountered by the present writer dealt with a north of England association established well before the 1980s to assist what were then referred to as 'coloured' people. It was apparently so close to the margins of financial viability that it took loans from its own tenants to purchase furniture, and eventually it was absorbed by a more established association. Recent events in the housing association world have confirmed the continuing vulnerability of some of the smaller organizations to disappearance or merger (see for instance reports in Black Housing, April/May 1993,p.5 and March/April 1994,p.3; see also Julienne, 1994). Dividing lines are sometimes drawn between larger associations, 'community based' ones, and co-ops, but the divisions are not always permanent or clear cut; management committees may be constituted differently in different types of associations, with a community based association perhaps including more tenants or prospective tenants (see Kingston, 1992). On the other hand some people running larger associations certainly see their organizations as having firm roots in local communities. For the purposes of our discussion we will use the idea of an association being community based fairly loosely, as a way of implying it has strong links with specific groups or localities.

Towards a commercial environment

During the late 1980s the Conservative government passed legislation and introduced new financial regimes for social rented housing. Housing associations - as we indicated above - were placed in a more prominent position in official social housing strategy. At the same time, however, the associations were encouraged to move in a more commercial direction; with the expectation that private finance should play a bigger part, and with an emphasis on so-called 'value for money' considerations (for comments on 'value for money' see Cameron and Soares, 1991). Increased involvement of private capital has produced a situation of 'mixed funding', in which associations rely on combining privately raised funds with Housing Corporation subsidy. In order to provide an adequate return on the private investment, household rents have had to be moved upwards. Rent levels are vulnerable to factors like changing interest rates, or development costs exceeding estimates.

For central government, securing value for money may primarily mean maximising numbers of new units provided for every pound of subsidy, or achieving lowest unit cost. Given the lack of concern in the UK for evaluating the indirect costs and benefits of public investment, notions of value for money have remained extremely crude. They appear to exclude ideas about taking account of potential gains from expenditure in terms of local community development. There are also possibilities that the new financial regimes and ideas on value for money have encouraged a decline in dwelling quality and standards, and perhaps even inhibited efforts to tackle design and planning issues in culturally sensitive terms. These could be effects of cost minimising strategies. In any event, the changes in the financial environment have disadvantaged smaller organizations with limited assets, and there have also been investment shifts away from housing rehabilitation schemes, 'expensive' inner city sites, and stress areas (Redman, 1992; Misra, 1990).[5] Lacking capital assets in terms of large stocks of dwellings, small new associations were expected to find it hard to raise funds in the private market on reasonable terms. Without stock, they seemed unlikely to be able to 'pool' rents or manage debt charges and running costs in ways that might help keep rents on newbuild schemes down to affordable levels.

The research basis for this chapter

This chapter is informed by material gathered during a series of specific research exercises at Leeds University from the late 1980s onwards. That work included an in depth case study of a charitable trust set up in Yorkshire to assist minority ethnic housing associations, a qualitative northern England survey of emerging black run and minority ethnic housing organizations, and a national study of the responses of white run housing associations to minority ethnic housing needs. It proved impossible to obtain funds for a comprehensive historical survey of the black voluntary housing movement, so our overview of events has had to be derived as a by-product of the specific funded projects, from analysis of the literature, and from contacts with selected key practitioner informants and a small number of researchers elsewhere. The amount of available detailed material on some aspects is therefore limited. Fortunately there is a new project, currently nearing completion at Manchester University, which will provide an up to date account of minority ethnic associations, and fill some of the gaps in research (see Todd and Karn, 1993 and 1994). In addition scholars can make use of the publications of the FBHO - notably the journal 'Black Housing', which is an invaluable source of ideas and information - and a growing number of reports elsewhere in the housing practitioner press (recent examples include Oke, 1993; Randall, 1994; Grenier, 1994; Nother, 1994a). Nonetheless, certain parts of our commentary are best treated as having an exploratory rather than definite status; it may eventually be necessary to qualify some of the interpretations. As far as parallels in other countries are concerned, only preliminary work has been possible to assemble comparative material. This has been through correspondence with researchers in a limited range of places;[6] see Appendix to this chapter.

Surprising developments within UK public policy?

As we noted in earlier chapters, central government's inner city funding policies have often been cast mainly in 'neutral' terms. Rather than targeting black people explicitly, programmes have been conceived of in terms of types of services or capital investment. In the 1980s, however, there was a surprising development in the direction of ethnic pluralism in one area of 'official' social policy in England, in social rented housing. This development may have relatively few equally significant counterparts at state or governmental levels elsewhere in 'developed' urban societies with histories of black migrant settlement.

The Housing Corporation's strategy

Although the 1980s was a period of Conservative government marked by retrenchment, and by attacks on state provision of funds and services, the Housing Corporation nonetheless embarked on a constructive new programme. This was to encourage, sustain - and if appropriate actually create - separate black run organizations as a channel for providing rented housing. Thus the Corporation began a five year programme for black and minority ethnic housing associations. Despite the exceptional nature of the Corporation's strategy, the new programme subsequently gained a substantial measure of political acceptance at national level.

There were a number of reasons for the initiative taken by the Housing Corporation. The strategy was a response to external pressures, but individual officials within the Corporation played a very important role through their commitment to innovation, and in translating intentions into firm practice. In the early 1980s public policy was faced with reacting to 'urban disturbances' which had occurred in many major towns and cities. There was also concern about housing from within the Commission for Racial Equality, and about 'race' from the National Federation of Housing Associations (NFHA). Furthermore, the activities of black housing specialists, and the emergence, growth and efforts of black led organizations - among them the Federation of Black Housing Organisations (FBHO) - were helping to put 'race' issues on the Corporation's agenda. There was a view that the performance of many white run housing associations had been poor as far as meeting the needs of minority ethnic communities was concerned, and that black people were under-represented amongst housing association staff. There was also concern that black people housed by white run agencies often had to face harassment without much understanding or support from their landlords.

The Housing Corporation reacted by adopting a more active general stance on 'race' equality; in effect a 'response package' was put in place. At the heart of the Corporation's new approach was to be the five year programme targeted on black and minority ethnic housing associations. This began in 1986/87, and involved resources for development of housing schemes, supplemented by revenue grants towards start-up and running costs. Before the decision was reached to create this programme, debate appears to have taken place within the

Corporation over issues of integration and segregation, funding, etc. One key participant explained to the present writer that although there was awareness of 'integrationist' arguments at the time, he took the view that development of black associations could be argued for as a necessary stage to be gone through, in order to give opportunities and managerial experiences to black people. It was essential that they were 'seen to be in charge of [their] own destiny', while growth of black run associations would help bring through people who would have impact on the wider voluntary housing management scene. In any event, individual senior officers and Board members seem to have been vital in securing acceptance for the strategy. A potentially difficult issue concerned implications for white run associations of any 'top slicing' of funds in the interests of their black run counterparts; clearly this would look less contentious at a time of general growth in funds than in periods of restraint. In general terms it seems that some senior officers and Board members were well aware of the unique nature of the programme, and indeed that some participants saw it as a 'jewel in the Corporation's crown' (or perhaps it was partly 'sold' internally in these terms).

The justification offered for the new programme in official statements has been that the programme was set up 'in response to reports by the National Federation of Housing Associations and other bodies which indicated that the housing needs of black and minority ethnic people were substantially worse than for other groups', and because people 'from ethnic minorities were also under-represented in every area of housing association work: committees, staff and lettings' (Housing Corporation, 1991). On the one hand housing associations were frequently receiving public funds for working in inner city areas where many black people lived, yet on the other hand black people appeared to play only a small role in management and to occupy an uncertain position as beneficiaries via lettings. In practical terms the five year programme was to mean devoting funds and staff effort to the tasks of promoting, registering and supporting specific organizations in areas of high black and minority ethnic population and housing need. Assistance and co-operation from established 'mainstream' associations, charitable funders, and local authorities would be desirable to help the programme succeed. The central objective was to encourage the development of black run and minority ethnic housing associations so that they could make a contribution to housing provision and management. Eventually they might hope to become financially viable, able to undertake their own housing development schemes, and reasonably autonomous.

Seen from the grass roots the strategy seemed to offer the possibility of control over lettings and management, a community input into design and planning, the opening up of certain job opportunities, and in due course the actual ownership of property in the form of dwellings belonging to an association. Undoubtedly, there were observers and participants at various levels who hoped that the new

89

strategy would help to facilitate speedier and wider involvement of black and minority ethnic people in the so-called 'mainstream' white dominated voluntary housing movement. Experienced housing activists were aware that some earlier efforts to establish new associations - catering primarily for so-called 'coloured people' - had ended in the absorption of these organizations in (or their changing into) mainstream 'white' associations (see Hancock, undated; Lemos, 1994,p.9). Housing activists were also in touch with the struggles of the small group of black run and minority ethnic associations and related bodies that were already up and running successfully. Consequently there was an awareness of some of the likely dangers and problems. Nonetheless, the new programme appeared to have considerable potential.

While the idea of black run associations was not an invention of the Housing Corporation, the five year programme did have an impressive impact; 44 black and minority ethnic housing associations were registered during the period. This brought the total number of these organizations that had secured a degree of formal recognition up to 63. The numbers of dwellings managed by these bodies remained small in relative terms at the end of the decade - 7,600 units owned or managed by early 1991 (Housing Corporation, 1991) - but their activities had been having an influence going well beyond their own development programmes. Some of their operations were leading the way in areas seen as complex for social provision (such as accommodation for Asian elders, for client groups with different language skills from the white population, etc.). The most dynamic ones were also having an influence on ideas and actions across the wider voluntary housing scene, nationally or locally. Fresh perspectives and new people were coming into some of the regional housing policy networks - sometimes individuals with no previous housing expertise - and an increased awareness began to develop amongst white managers in mainstream associations. In West Yorkshire, for example, a new charitable trust was established by the white run associations, with particular key individuals and the regional NFHA playing a leadership role. This was to support and assist the emerging black led organizations, and became a model subsequently adopted elsewhere (see Harrison, 1992d). These developments parallelled a very active role played in this field by a national body, the Housing Associations Charitable Trust (HACT), which provided grants and loans (see Harrison, 1991,pp.107-8). By the early 1990s quite a few of the leading white run developing associations had worked or were working alongside or in partnership with minority ethnic associations. These relationships developed further in the new decade, as formal development consortia began to become a larger feature on the housing association scene (Harrison, 1992a). Today some minority ethnic associations work with a very wide variety of partners and associates; a report on ASRA Greater London, for instance, indicates that it 'is currently working in 22 local authorities and with 32 housing association partners' (Grenier, 1994,p.28).

At grass roots level the new associations reflected considerable diversity in cultural terms, although the theme of responding to unmet housing needs was common to all. Some were especially interested in specific client groups such as older people, or sought to make a bridge between housing and social care. This tradition continues. There were also links with concerns about small businesses and community development in some places. In the wider housing scene, discussions of design matters related to religion and culture, and of site and dwelling issues related to security, were stimulated by the increased involvement of these diverse minority ethnic organizations (for instance see Patel, 1987; Penoyre and Prasad et al.,1993). To sum up on the first five year programme period, we can say that it gave impetus to changes in thinking in the housing association world which otherwise might have been much slower. At the same time it gave minority ethnic communities an opportunity of having more of a voice, and a place at the policy making table. With official encouragement several of the most dynamic black run associations grew rapidly. As the regional offices of the Housing Corporation attempted to implement the programme, local interest was stimulated. Establishing a registered minority ethnic association became a target for community leaders in many towns, and most large urban areas in England with substantial minority ethnic populations saw attempts to set up associations.

At the end of the five year period the Housing Corporation reaffirmed its commitment, publishing a second strategy document building on the initial programme and setting objectives for the next five years (Housing Corporation, 1992). The revised programme for 1991/92-1995/96 included plans for investing £750 million in schemes for creating over 12,000 new rented units, encouragement for white run associations to transfer about 2,400 existing dwellings to the minority ethnic associations, and creation of training programmes for some personnel in the small associations. The planned capital investment represented over 9% of the Housing Corporation's expected total investment in new programmes of rented housing (an increase from under 7% at the end of the previous decade). Revenue grant allocation was also to increase. Seen in isolation this looked like an extremely satisfactory outcome from the efforts of the movement and its allies.

Retreat and retrenchment

Unfortunately for black and minority ethnic communities, other changes in social housing made these gains somewhat insecure. The Corporation's supportive programmes had developed at a time when the housing association movement as a whole had begun to come under great pressure. In effect, a restructuring of social rented housing had been initiated towards the end of the decade. As the Conservative central government sought to achieve a variety of political and economic goals, ministers focussed on housing associations as well as local authority housing. Although housing associations were encouraged to take an enhanced role to displace local government housing departments, the associations were also being expected - as we noted above - to draw a greater part of their investment funds from the private sector. Rent rises for tenants were expected to follow logically from the revised funding/grant regimes, and housing renovation schemes and expensive new building projects in inner city areas became less feasible at the end of the 1980s. Small organizations (and perhaps their tenant clients) began to find the environment more difficult. Possessing as yet few assets in terms of housing units, most black run associations were likely to face severe obstacles as the era of mixed funding and increasing rents developed. Furthermore, trends seemed to point towards a scenario in which new development work eventually would be dominated by a relatively small number of the larger and more commercially strong associations. Few minority ethnic associations fell into this category, and some of the potential difficulties of the changed environment were being acknowledged by the Corporation when it carried out consultations prior to creating its strategy for the second five year period (see Housing Corporation, 1991). Reference was made then to the 'requirements for financial strength, viability and skill for all housing associations' being made 'more demanding' by changes introduced in national housing legislation in the 1988 Housing Act.

In this adverse financial climate the Housing Corporation continued to try to assist the black and minority ethnic associations, but the strategy took on a more selective character, and there was a shift in emphasis from promotion to consolidation. Selectivity of support was already on the agenda to some extent when the second five year programme was issued, but subsequently seemed to gather force in the first Corporation reviews of its strategy (which now take place annually). In the long run it seemed probable that economic constraints would set limits on the number of new associations expected to reach or maintain viability in terms of size, property holdings, and capacity to borrow private funds. From the Corporation's perspective, one way of making survival more likely for black run associations would be to encourage co-operation with established (larger) white run housing associations. Co-operation of this type was by no means new, but might imply a measure of dependency. It can mean that a significant share of available subsidies is helping to sustain the activities of the larger partner; and in some circumstances a black run association might even find difficulty in securing exactly the type of development it hoped for. Certainly some of the £750 million mentioned above would be channelled via white run partners. The

92

Corporation also encouraged inter-association housing stock transfers, which we also noted briefly above. This means passing some properties from ownership by a larger organization to a smaller one, as a potential means of securing asset growth for black run associations in the absence of large enough house building development programmes (see Misra, 1991). By various approaches, therefore, the Housing Corporation attempted to maintain momentum in the field, despite adverse funding regimes. When it was published, the 1992-96 strategy aimed at ensuring that 40 black and minority ethnic associations would become 'independent and effective organisations' over the new five year period.[7] The Corporation defined relevant associations as those 'established to meet the housing needs of ethnic minority people' and managed by a committee 'of which at least 80% are from the ethnic minority communities'; this referred to people who had 'African, Asian, Caribbean or South East Asian ethnic or racial origins'.

From late 1992 and through 1993 it appeared that the Corporation's slightly more selective but still essentially supportive stance was itself under stress, and the future of the revised programme was somewhat uncertain. Changes had been prompted by reduced housing association grant rates (meaning more dependence on private lenders), and a decreasing capital programme for the Housing Corporation. Various models for housing association development and funding were apparently being considered, and it seemed that the proposals would hit the smaller minority ethnic associations very hard if adopted. Some might face prospects of decline, delayed growth, merger with other associations, or a role as managing agents rather than as property owners. This would apply where a stronger (usually white run) partner association would retain the ownership of the stock. The trends were commented on very fully in the pages of 'Black Housing', which presented concerns about loss of independence, and the possibility of black run associations being turned into or merging with white run ones (see for instance Black Housing, June 1993, pp.8-11). As the FBHO's director put it at this time, 'Twelve months into the Housing Corporation's second five year strategy...and already the strategy is being shaken to its roots.' (Black Housing, editorial, February/March 1993). We can certainly note certain very significant policy shifts by the time of the Corporation's first annual review of its strategy for black associations (see Todd and Karn, 1993). First, registered black run associations were to be categorized into a number of distinct groups in accordance with judgements about their organizational strength and capacity to develop. The implication was that their status would vary, only some being perceived as appropriate vehicles for a full range of activities including initiation of their own housing developments. Second, perhaps the strategy would focus more on building the managerial base of black associations. Todd and Karn comment that 'Half the associations within the strategy will receive little development income, a vital source of revenue. They will also miss the

93

opportunity to learn the development skills, which would make them truly independent and viable' (p.9). These writers also suggested that one implication was that a shift towards establishing a small group of nationally based ethnic minority associations was now under way, meeting a need for a number of such associations that can compete for resources with other mainstream associations. This could be divisive; one 1994 press report referred to the 'big three' being accused of 'predatory actions', squeezing out smaller ethnic minority housing groups through competitive behaviour (Housing Associations Weekly, 379, 16 September 1994). By contrast, unregistered associations, and registered ones not seen as 'viable' enough to be developers, would have a role primarily as managing agents for dwellings. Some successful minority ethnic associations already act as developers for smaller ones (see for instance Randall, 1994,p.70), although more generally white run associations have had this development agent role.

In June 1994 the Housing Corporation approved a further review of the 1992-96 strategy (Housing Corporation, 1994). This provides an excellent point at which to conclude our discussion of Corporation strategies. It notes that capital allocations to black associations rose from £12 million in 1986/87 to £90 million in 1990/91; allocations from 1991 to 1994 totalled £426 million. The revenue grants budget (which included funding for black run associations) rose from £100,000 in 1986/87 to £600,000 in the 1986/87-1990/91 period. The minority ethnic associations are believed to own and manage 11,400 homes, with the expectation that this will rise to 17,500 by March 1996. Of the 63 black and minority ethnic associations registered with the Corporation, 38 at present 'participate in the strategy' along with 11 unregistered ones. Fourteen are seen as 'viable' at present, and on current projections a further 27 should achieve this by March 1996, with an additional 8 reaching viability within the following year. Nine associations have ceased to be part of the strategy because of 'problems in their performance or potential viability'. Interestingly, this recent review points out that the Corporation's black and minority ethnic housing associations strategy is itself perceived as nearing its end:

It is a Positive Action programme legitimised by the Race Relations Act 1976, which aims to rapidly bring about substantial and visible change to assist in meeting our race equality objectives. It is by this definition a temporary measure, and we are entering the final stages of this plan (Housing Corporation, 1994).

The Corporation is aware of the implications in terms of the measures that might be needed to consolidate the achievements so far, and 'has therefore begun to consider how it can continue to demonstrate its support for the development of black and minority ethnic associations after March 1996' (1994,p.4).

Concluding comments on developments since the late 1980s

Establishing new black run associations has proved by no means easy in the post-1988 context, although - despite the obstacles - the Housing Corporation remained committed to the task it had begun in the mid 1980s.[8] It is difficult to predict how matters will stand in 1996, at the end of the 1992-96 strategy period. The situation of many black run associations today is somewhat precarious, and it may be that only the largest of the black run associations will continue to be seen as appropriate vehicles for further development funding. New cultural groupings and communities seem unlikely to make the kind of headway that seemed feasible in the first five year period. Even so, there are still many unmet local needs, and places where the emergence or arrival of a black run association might fill important gaps, as in Glasgow (see Black Housing, January/February 1995, p.4).

On the positive side there has so far still been only limited visible racist 'backlash' against the Corporation's programme from amongst housing practitioners, official agencies, or established politicians. Black run and minority ethnic associations have not become a particular target for open abuse or hostile political campaigning. There have been some significant exceptions, as in a dispute in late 1991 over a housing development scheme for Tuntum Housing Association,[9] but such events seem to have created relatively few obstacles to implementation of the Corporation's strategy. Strong and overt local authority opposition to minority ethnic associations seems to have been the exception rather than the rule, with many councils being supportive, even though associations may experience 'outright racism from councillors' from time to time (see Connolly, 1993). At national level and in general terms financial obstacles have been more important than opposition from the political right. Advocates of an integrationist approach to social housing organizational development have not had a great deal of impact on the programme either. This is not to suggest that one should adopt a simplistic perspective on the political situation. Social housing itself is always likely to come under attack from certain parts of the UK political spectrum. One observer has gone so far as to argue that a 'witch-hunt' against such housing - especially that which serves minorities - is 'never far away' (Connolly, 1993,p.15). Nonetheless, racist hostility to the development of separate black run and minority ethnic housing organizations has not often surfaced in any very powerful or coherent form. On the other hand, mechanisms for judging capacity or evaluating performance can discriminate against certain kinds of organizations, and could even become vehicles for racist stereotyping.

The characteristics and activities of the black voluntary housing movement

We will first indicate some of the locations from which pressures for change are exerted by black and minority ethnic people in the UK housing field, and will note how the term 'black voluntary housing movement' tends to be used. Then attention will be paid directly to the FBHO, as the leading participant.

Challenges to public policy from within black and minority ethnic communities and from black housing professionals have been voiced through a range of independent channels. These channels have included local black run organizations concerned with community development, religion or welfare (including hostels). There have also been non-locally based organizations such as the FBHO, the Black Caucus, the Black Contractors Association, the Black Women in Housing Group, etc.[10] ('Black' is a word used inclusively in many instances, and therefore not necessarily implying only African/Caribbean.) In parallel with demands coming from such organizations, black and minority ethnic housing professionals have brought pressure to bear from within various white dominated agencies. Settings here have included the NFHA (which has remained extremely significant over a long period), some of the large established white run housing associations, certain local authority departments, etc. In addition there are some black activists directly engaged as local or national politicians with a commitment to advances in housing. Since there is often a sense of a shared effort being made for improvements by people in all these different settings, many might see themselves as involved in a movement for change. The important annual conferences hosted by the FBHO seem to attract a wide range of participants, and the terminology of a 'movement' is invoked regularly in relevant literature as well as in discussions. In practice the terms black voluntary housing movement and black housing movement tend to be employed in quite a flexible way, and sometimes apparently interchangeably. Even if the first of the two phrases is the narrower, the black voluntary housing movement nonetheless embraces a great variety of people and organizations making common cause for improvements in housing conditions. Participants may come from situations ranging from black run hostels with social service functions to black workers' groups formed within white run housing associations.

By the late 1980s it was the FBHO which had come to have the most significance amongst black run bodies in relation to national housing policies, and it continues to hold centre stage, although challenged from time to time (see for instance Housing Associations Weekly, 379,16 September 1994,p.7). Although it acts on behalf of many organizations and individuals, however, some minority ethnic or black participants in the housing association field do not have significant direct FBHO links. The point must be emphasized that the UK's black voluntary housing movement cannot be defined as a single political pressure

96

group or organized interest. It is much more than that. Even so, the existence of the FBHO has undoubtedly been crucial. It was founded in 1983, and offers a forum for discussion, a means of developing shared perspectives on issues, and a base from which pressure and innovation can come. The FBHO's journal, 'Black Housing', offers a chance to be heard for black organizations, and is in itself a significant voice and source of ideas on the British housing scene. The Federation has been much involved in the development of positive action initiatives in the field of housing staff training, trying to open up opportunities for potential new minority ethnic employees in housing associations and elsewhere. It also carries out consultancy, professional practitioner training, and research, as well as what might be seen as the key 'political' activity of making inputs into public policy formation processes. Although by no means a wealthy or entirely financially secure organization, the FBHO has during its development obtained significant funding from public sector agencies. It also acquires income by providing services and selling publications, and through membership fees, as well as seeking resources from charitable sources. One of its most important activities has been to help sustain, bring together, and encourage the black led housing associations that have developed in various English urban areas. Today it is probably the more effective of these organizations that make up the active 'heart' or strongest parts of the movement.

In the period leading up to the initiation of the Housing Corporation's five year programme, the FBHO seems to have become crucially important politically. The programme is probably best interpreted as having been the most significant part of a wider 'response package' on 'race' equality (see above). (Another component of the package was the Corporation's appointment of an in house 'race' adviser, a role that remained important). Earlier in this chapter we noted the active general stance adopted by the Corporation, and the vital role of some of its senior officers. Available information suggests that the FBHO was a major channel for mobilization of pressure on key officials leading to commitment to the changes, although recollections of informants now vary slightly over the Housing Corporation's interactions with the Federation. Certainly the idea for establishing black run associations was pursued strongly by the FBHO; a participant who played an important role within the Corporation at that time explained to the present writer that 'one always knew what they [FBHO] wanted'. This informant also argued, however, that 'tactically' they 'needed help' initially; nonetheless adding that although not experienced in dealing with statutory organizations, the FBHO 'became progressively more expert'. In addition, the Federation was soon drawn into a regular consultative relationship with the Corporation. Thus there was success in two obvious forms. Firstly, with its allies and supporters - outside and within the Corporation - the FBHO succeeded in securing strategic policy changes. Secondly, and despite being at that time relatively inexperienced, the Federation also acquired a place in policy formation processes.[11] Since then the FBHO has been consulted regularly over issues where it is seen as having an interest. Of course this does not mean that there is agreement with the Housing Corporation on all matters, or that the FBHO is perceived as the only channel for minority ethnic views, or that the Federation has ceased to be a severe critic of policies when necessary. Critical views in 'Black Housing' about recent trends in Corporation strategy indicate clearly that the FBHO is still a robust source of independent comment. Perhaps it has been less easy to be a fully consulted 'insider' in recent periods, however, than would have been the case if there had been a more favourable financial environment for social housing.

Incorporation

We now turn to the issue of 'incorporation', to consider the consequences of a relatively successful relationship between minority ethnic organizations and governmental agencies. Applying the notion of incorporation here primarily to refer to the process of 'drawing groups in', we can observe various more far reaching results from this process alongside the straightforward possibilities of day to day compromise or mutual accommodation. One possibility in the UK social housing field has been that the structures and purposes of independent organizations might be shaped in a particular direction as a result of emphases in public policy. This might happen both at national and local levels. For instance, a housing association rather than a co-operative organizational structure might be decided upon locally by community activists, because of the rules governing funding or financial viability. Or several culturally and ethnically diverse groups in a town might consider coming together to create one organization to bid for funding, instead of acting independently. This would be in order to improve the chances of success in the face of the preferences of the Corporation for strong client organizations. In our research materials there is local case study evidence of consequences of these kinds having occurred from time to time in the period of the first five year programme. More recently the possibility of mergers, alliances and group structures may have been given a heightened salience by the shifting financial and policy environment. Quite apart from the influence of the funding regimes, officials themselves have sometimes played a fairly direct role. At the regional offices of the Housing Corporation, in particular, this may have meant giving assistance and advice, exercising powers of persuasion, or acting in a 'brokerage' capacity; for example to help build connections between local minority ethnic housing bodies and more established white run ones. The Housing Corporation in any case has the responsibility to examine new organizations and their viability carefully before funding them. No association will become fully established - and obtain direct access to public funds - unless it can achieve formal 'registration' with the Corporation. To secure this recognition the new body must satisfy various criteria; once registered the association will also need to meet significant performance expectations. Although it would be a mistake to assume too simple a set of political relationships here, the Housing Corporation undoubtedly has held a powerful position in relation to individual associations (which in a sense become its clients when seeking recognition and funding). They may have been expected to demonstrate managerial or financial competencies, or to show how they could gain access to these things. This may have influenced committee memberships and character in some instances.

Turning to the funding arrangements and strategic planning at Housing Corporation headquarters, it is clear that priorities there directly influenced the programmes of new associations during the periods we have been looking at. This may well have distorted the development strategies of specific minority ethnic housing associations towards lower risk options, pragmatism and increased size, and away from prioritizing some of their original preferences. Opportunism and awareness of current Housing Corporation priorities could play a part, alongside a recognition that some locally preferred routes (such as developing large units on shared ownership tenure lines) were not financially feasible within current rules. Since growth and assets in terms of dwelling numbers seemed so important to continuing success, there were strong incentives for new associations to fall in with Corporation ideas. We are seeing here an obvious possible implication of a degree of incorporation into public sector agency strategies and networks: that policy goals decided elsewhere may influence the movement strongly. There has been an impact not only on local organizational development, but on housing scheme development choices. This consequence has arisen partly because there is rationing of the limited public funds available. Yet there is an even more fundamental way of looking at the issues. The Housing Corporation's role is primarily about spending public money to generate specified kinds of housing development outcomes. Viewed from the perspective of community activists, therefore, what is available is a housing development programme in terms of monies to be bid for. Periodic attempts to secure allocations of funds take on great importance. An effort to obtain funding can only be made if the right kind of organization can be built up. It must appear credible in terms of committee membership (and include appropriate expertise), and may be better placed if it can call upon local supporters among other more established housing agencies. In due course registration with the Corporation as a recognised housing association becomes an important objective, because without this there can be no independence and possession of properties. Furthermore, the housing plans of the newly created black run organization may be adjusted to fit with the priorities of the Corporation at that particular time. Thus there is considerable pressure exerted on the form and behaviour of organizations by the opportunities to develop and obtain resources. As one informant explained in an interview with the present writer, activities are 'actually funding-led' rather than 'needs-led'. This is not to deny the continuing importance of grass roots knowledge and pressure in influencing perceptions in official agencies and white run associations, but there is a two way process of influence taking place.

While the account we are giving here may oversimplify, the general contention of the argument is firmly founded. In drawing in and giving recognition to housing associations as potential recipients of public subsidies in the period from the mid 1980s, the Housing Corporation exerted a substantial influence not only on types or numbers of houses, but also on organizational development and purposes within communities. This type of process may well have occurred previously with white run associations, and with black led specialized needs organizations in slightly different contexts.

So far we have been discussing the impact that contact with the Housing Corporation may have had on individual housing associations. This needs to be supplemented by observations about the FBHO, and the ways in which it may have been influenced by the development of the five year programme and a successful relationship with public policy. The FBHO reacted during the 1980s in various ways to the challenges of building links with and helping to support and mobilize a changing constituency of organizations. The Director was certainly keen to make contact with emergent organizations up and down the country. A north of England office was established in Liverpool at the end of the decade, countering any possible charge that the FBHO might be a rather London orientated body. Later, the Federation established a Council of Black Housing Associations, made up of representatives from black and minority ethnic associations, while a policy adviser was appointed at the FBHO with Housing Corporation support.[12] A reasonable interpretation of these two particular steps is that they were fairly direct responses to requirements generated by the Corporation's strategy for black and minority ethnic associations. Another issue is the character of the FBHO itself; one of the present writer's informants felt that the Federation was today more definitely a housing orientated organization than it had been in its early period.

Perhaps the central role which the Federation holds within the black voluntary housing movement is owed partly to the organization's success in working alongside the Corporation in the early years, partly to successful adaptation to the changing housing policy scene since then, and partly to the recognition that the FBHO still receives in official circles. Problems may arise today insofar as the changing financial climate may have reduced the potential value or seriousness of consultations with representative housing organizations. If there is less manoeuvrability for Corporation officers because of funding cuts and changed regimes, then consultation perhaps appears less meaningful, possibly making complaints or divisions more likely within the movement. A report in Housing Associations Weekly, for instance, refers to claims of disillusion 'with FBHO,... the Council of Black Housing Associations... and the NFHA's working group on black associations'; apparently the FBHO is 'doing some very good work', but 'not getting the channels into the Housing Corporation or government' (see 379,16 September 1994,p.7). On the other hand consultations with the FBHO do continue, as well as with associations at regional levels, etc.

Representation and solidarity

Being a federation means that the FBHO maintains legitimacy as the representative of member organizations. There can sometimes be problems in maintaining solidarity across perceived ethnic boundaries. It appears that the term 'Black' can be in itself a point of difficulty here for some UK housing activists. A minority ethnic organization may not necessarily wish to attach this terminology to itself, even though the members of that organization are experiencing the consequences of white racism. Common action under a black banner may therefore be difficult. Our research in northern England also found that gender had been a focus for some dissent. This is not really surprising. Religious or cultural issues are very important to some of the new associations, and there may be a strong cultural predisposition in some places to conceive of women and men as having very different functions and characteristics. Thus a researcher may come across a 'traditional' view that would place women in the home (or restricted private circle) rather than as association committee members attending as individuals in their own right or as representatives of community interests. It is difficult to generalize here (and in any case charges of gender bias could equally well be directed at a number of white run associations). Working against this kind of factor is the need for new associations to respond politically to the Housing Corporation, local authorities and other agencies. This provides a strong incentive to seek a united front, to participate in the FBHO, to make an acknowledgement of equal opportunities needs, and to construct links with other minority ethnic housing organizations. Perhaps the response on an issue such as gender sometimes may contain a degree of tokenism on the part of the minority ethnic organization (just as it may with some white run associations on gender or 'race'). On the other hand there is also some increase in consciousness of good practice on equal opportunities; because of entry into housing networks, contact with the Federation, etc. As far as national and regional mobilization is concerned, the FBHO itself undoubtedly seeks to represent and act for a

101

constituency including people of varied cultural or ethnic backgrounds and outlooks. In the present writer's view the Federation has achieved a remarkable degree of success in trying to do this, despite the problems.

Movements, empowerment, and individuals

This chapter has described some recent events in Britain which look surprising in the context of the Thatcher years. We have indicated how pressure was exerted in the housing field by and on behalf of black people, and how a measure of success was achieved in the 1980s and early 1990s. Alongside these gains we have recorded the impact that interactions had on the form, directions and scope of the black voluntary housing movement itself. It was to a degree conditioned; by official strategies, by funding regimes, and by priorities and commitments within Housing Corporation offices, local authority departments and established housing associations. From a theoretical perspective what stands out is the *close relationship between an important social welfare movement and the institutions of the state*. Political and bureaucratic responses to dissent have taken form alongside and in a clear relationship with the emergence and development of the social movement itself. Power derived from managing access to resources has meant that state agencies and official goals have affected the social movement strongly. This has extended to *an influence on the characteristics of minority ethnic housing organizations themselves* at local level; on their scope, geographical distribution and form. In influencing access to and distribution of gains to households, *the detail of institutional mechanisms for providing and funding social housing is very important*. There are specific elements in the ensemble of policies and practices which can be shaped by demands pursued on behalf of interests at the grass roots. As we have seen, an effectively represented but broad social welfare movement certainly can have an impact. Nonetheless, empowerment of communities and households may remain limited. This is likely if it is within a residualized and selectivist setting, where funds are vulnerable to swift reduction by politicians, and in a context where housing investment is treated in isolation both from its indirect effects and from questions of low income. Looked at in broad terms, *state management of consumption helps create ground on which collective actions can take place*, and where solidarities may be forged. *To move from action to being genuinely empowered, however, requires control of assets* on a secure basis.

Most of our discussion has focussed on a broad movement and some of its constituent parts, but has not very directly considered the issue of consumer empowerment in terms of individual tenants or other local residents. It is time to explore the situation for individuals as well as for larger groupings, dealing with

102

benefits and then with limitations and constraints. In effect we will be reviewing how far the success of the black voluntary housing movement has been able to bring about a strong measure of empowerment.

Achieving empowerment for communities and individuals

Collective struggles to secure a voice and a seat at the policy making table have benefited minority ethnic communities in terms of influence on events, opportunities for black professionals, and so forth. Creation of a minority ethnic housing association may also greatly benefit tenants. They may be covered by the Housing Corporation's Tenants' Guarantee, which confers certain rights [13], but this is not the same as having a good relationship with the landlord. One of the assertions made about small associations with local roots is that they are better able to respond to community needs, and will create more of a participatory environment than larger organizations. A feature notable in the development of black run associations has been their potential to reflect neglected community needs and voices, and the situation in their housing therefore may contrast sharply with the prospects for minority ethnic participation elsewhere in social rented housing (see comments by Clarke in Cooper, 1991). In some respects minority ethnic associations see themselves as reflecting and responsible to fairly specific constituencies, able to offer a culturally sensitive service, identifying unmet needs, and with an image of shared experiences, language, or religion on the part of staff and potential tenants (see for instance points in Jones, 1994,pp.9,82-6; cf Lemos, 1994,p.5). It is in these senses that the black run housing associations have often been perceived as potentially empowering. They may *facilitate both anti-racist practices and cultural pluralism*, and this has helped generate support from within communities.

Another notable characteristic of the black voluntary housing movement has been the capacity to make connections between housing as shelter on the one hand, and social care, community development and employment on the other. Pioneering projects have demonstrated that some associations have the capacity to develop complementary non housing projects which may benefit some of their most disadvantaged tenants (Julienne in Nother, 1994). Some minority ethnic associations have also been in the forefront of efforts to encourage local black run businesses.

Limitations and constraints

There are many difficulties in achieving empowerment through a housing association. *First*, there are *implications of size, growth, and managerialism*. In

103

the commercialized environment of today it is easier for large associations to thrive. Nother states that the largest 88 NFHA members now own 65 per cent of housing association stock (Nother, 1994). A big association can probably offer a very professionalized service to tenants in many respects, and may even be able to have relatively low rents. On the other hand questions may arise about its sensitivity, accountability and objectives. Furthermore, for housing associations as for many other kinds of organizations, growth can seem to be an end in itself. Some smaller associations have felt strong pressure to grow through development or acquisition of stock. Todd and Karn (1994) suggest that for minority ethnic associations this has sometimes meant prioritizing property development rather than working out the implications for management. Associations which relied previously on informal approaches derived from grass roots networking may need to create more organized tenant consultation and participation processes. If an association is to continue a tradition of cultural sensitivity in management and planning as it grows, it will need to seek systematic feedback. Genuine participation is an essential aspect of empowerment. This may require tenants to feel that they have a measure of effective 'ownership' of the organization and what it does, and strong representation on the voluntary management committee; but this in turn may be problematic or face obstacles (in relation to potential conflicts of interest, corruption, or charitable status; see Nother, 1994,p.12). The situation might be more straightforward in some kinds of co-operative housing organization, but co-ops have found difficulty in making headway in the UK. Most housing associations have a degree of division between managers and managed, even though tenants may be represented at committee level. The empowerment black run associations offer will be of less value if they do not continue to connect closely with their roots. This danger - heightened by commercial pressures - is captured in one view from critics within the black voluntary housing movement; that some organizations might eventually become 'white housing associations with black faces' (see letter from Soares to Voluntary Housing, February 1993,p.9).

NFHA member housing associations generally claim to see accountability to tenants as more important than accountability to anyone else, but are not all necessarily strong advocates of tenant power (Kearns, 1994). Indeed Kearns notes that 'there is little appetite for making associations locally accountable in "grass roots" terms', and there are 'low levels of support for the formal involvement in associations' affairs of prospective tenants and the local community'(p.10). He reports that accountability to private lenders received a higher rating among NFHA members surveyed than did direct accountability to the 'local community' (defined as residents other than tenants and prospective tenants). The collective empowerment we are concerned with might be undermined by any rift between managers and localities, but the situation in black run associations might be different here from in a large white run one. At the heart of the problems for potential tenants, however, lies the issue of access to resources over which they can exert a measure of influence; clearly this might require that local 'ownership' or control of assets was not over-diluted in the interests of financial institutions, other lenders, or local authority nomination rights (see Soares, 1993).

Second, there are potential *problems of continuing consumer disadvantage in situations of restricted resources*. Offsetting the advantages for tenants noted earlier could be the possibility of an imprisoning situation of higher rents and little choice, for black people who remained inhibited about using other social housing suppliers. In a sense a new 'dual market' might even develop (similar to one found sometimes in the private sector), in which black people became accustomed to approaching only specific associations which catered deliberately for them (although also catering for some other tenants). Yet their associations would have limited stock on offer and rents which might sometimes be higher than average. To some extent the scenario for tenants here is bound to depend on the financial environment facing black run associations, whether they can acquire more varied ready built stock through transfers, and the degree of racism experienced when tenants try to move elsewhere. Money is crucial for the pursuit of both tenants' and associations' strategies. In chapter 2 we noted the difficulty of inserting genuine empowerment into situations of severe poverty, resource constraints and disadvantage; this will set limits on what can be achieved for some tenants even where they have culturally sensitive landlords. At the same time precariousness of funding is evidence of the vulnerability of targeted selectivist systems of support by contrast with more universalistic ones.

Third, some clients may have property aspirations that are difficult to meet; in particular *the wish to become owners*. Property rights - and the capacity to use them in a way that accommodates participatory processes - can appear a crucial route to genuine influence and control for groups and communities, and we have already referred to the idea that tenants may need a sense of ownership. Going further, however, alongside tenants we need to consider potential owner-occupiers. Shared ownership schemes offer one route for housing associations to assist the strategies of households that wish to buy. Some housing associations have confronted difficulties in this field (see Hale, 1992; Lemos, 1994,p.61), and it may be an area where black households have not yet benefited greatly. Perhaps their requirements cannot be met readily in this form, given low incomes. On the other hand the issue has been highlighted recently in London by the creation of Pamoja, a new initiative between Ujima Housing Association and Notting Hill Home Ownership. This aims at giving minority ethnic households increased access to shared ownership homes.

Fourth, there are questions on the feasibility of being able to link housing with other concerns, despite what we said above about the capacity to do so. One relates to *the extent to which social housing investment and its indirect benefits might be controlled or exploited locally* for the benefit of small firms, employment or training. This issue interests white run organizations too, and ideas have appeared about some housing associations becoming local development agencies (Wadhams, 1992). This could be a direct approach to community empowerment. On the other hand there has been little accommodation of these concerns by central government in its grants and legal arrangements. There are also doubts about the continuing *governmental compartmentalization of housing and social services,* which may inhibit black run agencies that would like to work across the housing/care/economic development boundaries.

Notes

1. Some of the material presented here has been referred to previously in journal and conference papers, although along different lines. I am grateful to editors and referees - including those at the Canadian Journal of Urban Research and the journal Critical Social Policy - for giving me the opportunity to develop my ideas in print, and I would like to thank seminar participants at CSP and SPA conferences who commented helpfully in discussions.
2. The best introduction to Conservative policy objectives in the late 1980s is Secretaries of State for the Environment and Wales, 1987.
3. Some percentage figures for households were given in chapter 4, indicating the relative significance of local authority and housing association stocks, and their housing of minority ethnic households.
4. Local authorities have had a history of giving support too, and the supply of potential sites from this source has been important. See also Harrison, 1991a.
5. Material on the impact of the new regimes is given in JRF, 1992a, 1992b.
6. Although the writer's comparative research has not progressed far, it suggests that UK experience is distinctive.
7. Housing Corporation, 1992,p.1. Independent here is intended to mean that the associations should no longer be dependent upon public revenue grants for funding their 'core' activities and overheads expenditures.
8. 'Race equality' was probably considerably higher on the Corporation agenda by the end of the 1980s than in 1979. Perhaps this resulted at least partly from political pressure and achievements during the detailed discussion of

new social housing legislation. Sarre, Phillips and Skellington refer to parliamentary activity in connection with the legislation, and to involvement of the FBHO, CRE and NFHA. These authors note rejection in parliament of all the proposed anti-racist amendments, 'except one seeking to bring the Housing Corporation under the aegis of Section 71 of the 1976 Race Relations Act (thus requiring them to promote racial equality)' (see 1989,p.353). This change was followed by the Corporation conferring on associations via circular the duties to eliminate unlawful discrimination and promote equality of opportunity.

9. A few such cases of conflict have been reported in the general housing press or national newspapers. This particular one provided interest for newspapers partly because of involvement by a prominent national politician, and the fairly explicit racism that critics felt was being voiced. One local white politician is recorded as having expressed opposition to the allocation of houses in his area by a black run association with the sentence, 'We do not wish to see Rushcliffe becoming a dumping ground for dross'. See The Guardian, November 22 1991; and comment by Louis Julienne in Black Housing, December 1991,p.13. Also cf East London experience reported in Housing Associations Weekly, 64, 29 April 1988,p.16.

10. Information on organizations and their campaigns is scattered. Little research has been carried out on the Black Caucus in housing (which no longer operates). For an outline of *collective activities by black women* see comments in Dhillon-Kashyap. She gives information on black women's efforts to organize their own provision (1994, pp.122-4), including refuges. See also Rao, 1990,p.2. The *Black Contractors Association* has been primarily a London based organization which tries to press for improvements in the situation facing black run businesses in the construction field. It has also provided a forum for these businesses. *Architects and consultants* have organized. A circulated newsletter from the Society of Black Architects describes their first open meeting in June 1990. Amongst the contents are: a statement that 'Black' is intended to include Asian and other people of non European descent as well as African and Afro-Caribbean people; a warm welcome for the setting up of the group from the Association of Black People in Planning; and reports on the discussions at the meeting (SOBA Newsletter 1, 18 July, 1990). For a useful recent report see Bulgin, 1995.

11. N.B. The FBHO's Director was an interviewing panel member for the appointment of the Corporation's first housing and 'race' adviser.

12. Housing Associations Weekly, 281, 18 September 1992. The CBHA was to be elected, with one representative from each Housing Corporation region.

13. See Housing Corporation, 1989; and 'Board to consider Tenants' Guarantee changes', Corporation News, 39,October 1994.

APPENDIX: Comparative housing experiences

Since the empowerment of disadvantaged housing consumers is a topic of concern in many parts of the world, it seemed likely that there might be parallels elsewhere for UK experiences, perhaps especially in the USA. Enquiries through correspondence (mostly in 1991-93) were met with generosity by a number of scholars and practitioners, and this has made possible some comments on Australia and North America below. So far, however, no further more systematic research has been feasible, and no material has been gathered for continental western Europe. Also, the accounts below might be subject to correction if the writer has misinterpreted information, or where the position has changed recently.

In *Australia* there is a programme called 'CHIP', the Community Housing and Infrastructure Program. This is run by the Aboriginal and Torres Strait Islander Commission (ATSIC) to help the minority ethnic population through better housing and improved living conditions. There is also a Community Development Employment Program (CDEP). The Commission provides grant funds through CHIP to Aboriginal and Torres Strait Islander organizations on the recommendation of ATSIC Regional Councils. As in the British case, some self management is involved, and the houses are generally for renting (although there is a home purchase incentive scheme for households). The recipient organization normally owns the houses that are purchased or constructed, but some organizations permit sales of dwellings to tenants. Since the funding of community based Aboriginal and Torres Strait Islander organizations for housing purposes has apparently been taking place since the early 1970s, it is likely that in many senses Australia may be well in advance of the UK in this field. On the other hand this is a set of policies to assist populations that are the original resident groups, rather than ethnic minority ones created by migration into a white dominated society. A comprehensive review has recently been carried out of the Aboriginal and Torres Strait Islander housing organizations (see KPMG Management Consulting, 1994). Amongst the issues covered was home ownership, and tenants' interest in purchasing their dwellings.

In *Canada* there is useful information on migrant households, tenant organizations, and landlord/tenant relationships available in studies supported by the Canada Mortgage and Housing Corporation (TEEGA Research Consultants, 1983; Prairie Research Associates, 1991 and 1991a). The Corporation has also helped support work to create a catalogue of Canadian housing and shelter organizations (Pinsky and D'Sousa, 1988). This included (in the late 1980s) nine organizations related to immigrants (or refugees) only, and 26 related to native people only. The nine orientated to migrants covered a range of services - counselling and referral, information, related social services, advocacy, community development, legal services, etc. - and in some instances targeted specified groups (such as women, children, youth, and so forth). Amongst those listed for native Canadians was the Inuit Non-Profit Housing Corporation, and other agencies with a housing focus (such as improved rural housing).

Canada has a non-profit co-operative housing sector, which includes about 65,000 housing units owned by over 1,500 co-ops. The residents are the co-op members, who decide on the planning, design and day to day management. The governments of Canada, the provinces and some municipalities have provided assistance. The Co-operative Housing Federation of Canada (the umbrella body) does not have any publications dealing directly with black run or minority ethnic housing, but does have some multicultural co-ops in different cities across Canada. These may house members of one minority ethnic group and sometimes people from differing ethnic backgrounds. Information from Canadian scholars and from Lyse Huot of the Co-operative Housing Federation certainly indicates that there is independent or voluntary activity targeted on housing minority ethnic groups or 'New Canadians' in major cities, although not necessarily along the same lines as in the UK's Housing Corporation programmes. More than 25 co-ops have apparently grown out of the needs of migrant groups, etc., including South East Asian, Spanish, Filipino, Ukrainian, and German people. At the same time efforts to organize and self manage within public sector housing have occurred, and this could be relevant in any comparison of housing empowerment for black tenants. Canadian scholars also indicate that innovative moves have been made by some provincial governments recently (towards self help programmes, etc.).

An excellent introduction to the minority ethnic housing scene in *the USA* is provided by contributions from Leigh (1991). Material on relevant initiatives (including mutual housing associations) may be found also in Harloe and Martens, 1990. Federal government involvement has taken varied forms, some unfamiliar in the UK. For instance, federal housing subsidy programmes in the late 1980s included the Nehemiah Housing Opportunity Grants Program, which established a revolving loan fund providing money to non profit organizations to make loans to moderate income families purchasing homes developed by these 'non profits' under the programme. Housing was to be concentrated in given neighbourhoods in an effort to rebuild depressed areas of cities, and the programme was apparently similar to a state fostered Nehemiah programme previously developed and operated by church groups in Brooklyn (Leigh, 1991,p.250; see also Harloe and Martens, 1990,pp.94-9). It is possible some parallels might be discovered in certain initiatives with UK experience, although in very different contexts. Importantly, legislation in 1974 established the Community Development Block Grant (CDBG) programme to consolidate a wide range of community development activities directed toward neighbourhood revitalization, economic development, and improved community facilities and services (Leigh, 1991,pp.246-7). Revitalization could include either rehabilitation or substantial reconstruction of housing.

Contacts with US scholars suggest that most black led non profit housing in recent years is likely to have been carried out through Community Development Corporations (CDCs). James Tickell, from the UK, investigated community developers (including CDCs) under the auspices of a Harkness Fellowship. He notes that many such developers are based 'in racially mixed or black areas' (1992,p.12). He also comments on problems of high rents and affordability, the 'imperative to develop' to satisfy funders (p.45), and the difficulties of reconciling community accountability with business efficiency (p.48). Taub has raised interesting questions about implications for empowerment, suggesting that representation of community residents on CDC boards 'does not cut very deeply' (1990,p.8). Vidal (1992) has produced a national study of urban CDCs, and covers their variety, community connections or roots, neighbourhood focus, staffing, etc. Their scale appears to be modest, but they are complex. 78 per cent of those sampled had received federal funds, most commonly from the CDBG programme (p.3). Vidal notes that their 'largest single program area' had been housing, but that decline in funding had affected them; many CDCs appeared unable now to produce housing for people with very low incomes (p.4). In some ways there may be parallels with UK experiences, but CDCs may engage in activities that include commercial real estate development and business enterprise development as well as housing. The 'activity mix shifts' as circumstances change (p.5). Where the CDC focus is not on a geographical neighbourhood, a 'specific demographic group' may be targeted, and this may be 'along ethnic lines' (p.38). Vidal's figures for composition of CDC boards indicate the presence of residents or 'clients', alongside community based organizations, religious leaders, professionals, bankers, etc.(p.39). Unfortunately, no research information was obtained by the present writer on black led Community Development Corporations.

As far as could be ascertained (in 1991-92), there had been no direct US parallel with the UK Housing Corporation's programmes for minority ethnic housing associations; federal programmes did not appear to have targeted organizational growth in the same explicit way. Nonetheless there had been routes through which black run organizations could obtain public funds, and also housing co-operatives and other bodies which might manage housing for black people. For public sector schemes, tenant management and empowerment have been on the political agenda, sometimes linked not only with self management but also with privatization (see Jacobs, 1992,p.249; Tickell, 1992,p.38) .

6 Social housing investment and community development

At the end of the 1980s, during fieldwork on social housing organizations, the present writer was sometimes able to visit schemes that were in progress on specific inner city sites. It was a surprise to find on more than one occasion that the on-site workforce seemed to be entirely composed of white men, although the dwellings were likely to be let to minority ethnic households on completion. This highlighted an issue that was being mentioned at that time by activists from minority ethnic communities, and which remains important for inner city residents today. It concerns the allocation of jobs and contracts, and the impact of property development schemes on local people's opportunities.

Arguments about the merits of inner city capital investment in terms of urban regeneration often rely partly on the assumption that the main beneficiaries will be local people and businesses. Yet it is extremely hard to demonstrate that the indirect effects of investment have substantially helped inner area communities or entrepreneurs, either through long term job creation or increased demand for services or products. This matter - which relates to distributive outcomes - has already been touched on in chapter 3. In the social housing field there have been no reliable and systematically collected data on this issue. While black people have increasingly been seen as potential clients as far as housing association lettings are concerned, critics have argued that black run businesses have lost out in the distribution of other benefits from the investments. Thus there has been talk about black run firms failing to obtain housing scheme contracts, and white workers being ferried in to take the jobs on sites in areas where minority ethnic populations are large. Claims have been made that few black run companies or minority ethnic tradespeople have shared in the benefits from newbuild, repair or maintenance contracts. It has also been argued that few suppliers of goods or consultancy services have been black. Meanwhile the white run firms which dominate building activity are said to be unlikely to employ black workers or subcontractors. These topics have been considered from time to time by individual housing associations, the National Federation of Housing Associations, local authority departments, and concerned practitioners, and in May 1987 the Federation of Black Housing Organisations held a day seminar on the issues.[1] Yet still the topic remained unresearched. Academic and professional literature has covered these concerns about the impact of investment from time to time, but 'hard data' have been difficult to find.

Housing associations as a focus for research

One important potential focus for research would clearly be housing associations. The associations might be thought to possess some leverage in this area, given the amount of work they commission; with some capacity to influence employment practices within white run firms, and to employ black run ones. In recent years, while much of the house building sector has been stagnating or declining (including local authority newbuild), the associations have continued to grow. Growth in the 1980s might have meant many new opportunities for black run firms to enter the field, with housing associations offering encouragement.

In a survey carried out in 1991, however, the present writer found only limited evidence of effective efforts in this sphere. This was despite the fact that the chief foci of the research were the significant developing associations, which were frequently well aware of many equal opportunities questions. It was hard to find concrete evidence of many substantial and lasting successes in using a range of black contractors. The most widespread type of initiative was involvement by associations in the establishing of registers or directories of firms. In London and Birmingham registers had been created with the intention of improving awareness and communications, and helping businesses get the chance of housing association work (we include more comment on registers below). Beyond this kind of approach, some associations had had records of involvements with unemployed people, with workshops, with skills training, with urban renewal enterprises, etc. Joint activity with Task Forces or other local agencies was noted in a small number of instances of ad hoc projects or initiatives, or for particular development schemes. On a more modest level, active recruitment of contractors had been pursued in a variety of ways. Despite such efforts, there was nonetheless a sense of limitations, obstacles, inadequacies in association policies, or a difficult context. In some places, respondents stated, few minority ethnic firms were up and running, and those that were might be experiencing difficulty in competing for work against longer established firms. Monitoring of the activities of contractors seemed difficult. It seemed that black led firms were more likely to be found in maintenance and small scale renovation

112

work than in larger contracts. A few of the questionnaire replies suggest the mood amongst housing association personnel in 1991:

'To date there has been little success in this area';
'We have produced several reports and recommendations but little progress has been made in this area';
'Specific targeting of black contractors with very limited success';
'This is an area where we have probably been least successful, in common with most housing associations and local authorities'.

This survey - supported by the Joseph Rowntree Foundation - was successful in terms of response rate and coverage. 152 complete or nearly complete questionnaire replies were obtained, against seven less complete responses and eight refusals or non responses (see Harrison, 1992c,p.4, for a fuller account). It was not based on percentage sampling, but tried to cover all the relevant associations above a certain size in England. Consequently the somewhat negative impression on this topic seemed unlikely to result from an accident of sampling or response (cf CRE, 1993,pp.56-60). The contractors issue, however, formed only a small part of a larger investigation, and could only be dealt with in a preliminary way in 1991. More research would be needed to get a firmer picture.

Case study research

Again with the support of the Joseph Rowntree Foundation, the 'Race' and Public Policy (RAPP) research unit at Leeds carried out a fuller investigation on this neglected research topic in 1993/94 (see Harrison and Davies, forthcoming 1995). This was in the context of a broader research initiative by the Foundation in the construction industry field.[2] For our own project RAPP's approach was to develop a set of case studies of housing associations, complemented later by case work on individual building and contracting firms run by black or minority ethnic people. Much of the fieldwork was carried out by Jacqui Davies, who managed to establish excellent rapport with officers and businesses in what is a difficult field to research. (She was so successful that we had virtually no non responses from contacts in the field.) The project focussed on experiences in six English cities, and looked at the performance of twenty case study housing associations spread across these locations. To this we added case studies with fifteen contracting firms and tradespeople, to obtain perspectives which would complement the housing association viewpoints.

Findings based on case studies often need to be approached carefully, given the limitations of representativeness and of variety in the selection and coverage undertaken. The associations selected, however, were all felt to have relatively high profiles on equal opportunities issues, so that any negative findings about their performance could be expected to understate what might be found in less committed associations and across the housing association movement as a whole. In one city the research achieved a fuller picture by including all the main local housing association 'actors' involved in the areas of minority ethnic settlement, as well as a freestanding care and repair scheme working in these locations. The fifteen contractors were selected to provide a reasonable range of useful examples and experiences, but were not meant to be representative in any more strictly statistical sense. There was no time for the research to include in a systematic way consultancy services or the supply of goods, so our findings relate essentially to building firms and trades. Some specific work was also carried out on the efforts that have been made in a number of places to develop initiatives to improve opportunities for minority ethnic firms to compete effectively for housing association work (the registers in particular).

In overall terms, the research project can be regarded as having been exploratory rather than definitive, being designed to raise and explore issues and themes, but not to provide a complete overview. Nonetheless, some of our findings were disturbing from the point of view of urban regeneration and local community development. The main results - including options for improved practices - will be outlined below under four headings, and we will then summarize and draw some conclusions.

Housing associations and their relationships with firms

Housing associations sometimes may employ their own 'in house' maintenance staff, but on the whole they tend to commission outside contractors to take on the maintenance and repair jobs. At the smallest levels of expenditure there is likely to be an element of officer discretion in recruiting and using firms and tradespeople, but managerial and committee approval will normally be needed for any substantial contracts. As far as we could determine, the use of 'approved lists' of contractors is widespread and normal as a method of establishing and vetting a pool of acceptable firms on which to draw. Thus a firm seeking housing association work will usually need to gain a place on the approved list in order to be able to bid or tender for jobs. Entry to the list may depend on satisfying criteria laid down by the association to protect its investment and the quality of work; this is a factor that can be an obstacle to a new or inexperienced firm. There are variations around the practice of using lists; for example, in one case

114

we found an association using a minority ethnic firm on a provisional or trial basis although the firm was not yet on the approved list. There can also be variations in how competitive the process of awarding contracts is. An association may negotiate with one or more firms, rather than using open competition, or may prefer to employ a few tried and trusted tradespeople rather than inviting many bids for the work. Negotiation could be seen as a way of helping a new locally based firm get established as an effective participant. Generally, however, there is an assumption that a degree of competition will occur, perhaps especially where substantial sums are involved. This means that contractors not only need to be on the approved list so as to be invited to tender, but also require a good understanding of housing association practices, the pricing of jobs, etc., in order to have a chance of making a realistic bid.

For contracts in the field of 'development', many of the same points apply, except that the scale of jobs is often likely to be large, so that only well resourced firms may be able to consider bidding at all. There may be a 'design and build' approach needed in some instances, whereby a full package of services and skills is to be offered by the contractor tendering for a large newbuild scheme. Nonetheless, associations appear to use approved lists for development work in a rather similar way to their use of repair/maintenance lists. Sometimes a clear distinction is not drawn between the approved lists for development and repair/maintenance, but in many instances the lists are used separately. One important additional feature of housing association practice is that often - as far as we can tell - very little intervention occurs in the selection and appointing of subcontractors. This seems to be left up to the main contractor in many instances, rather than the association seeking to nominate firms or tradespeople. Consequently there will be some reliance on networks of contacts and customary practices amongst the larger builders themselves. Clearly this may cut against the entry of new tradespeople and against equality of opportunity, if established networks are strong and exclusive.

Given the framework of approved lists described above, an association has a number of options for recruiting. It can be passive, waiting to be approached by firms that know about housing associations and are seeking entry to lists. In these circumstances the lists will probably alter only very slowly. The association may primarily rely on tradespeople who have been used successfully in the past (and are on a list already), and rarely review the composition of its lists in a thoroughgoing way. This kind of situation will often make it likely that long established white run firms will dominate in the allocation of jobs. Alternatively, a housing association can be more proactive, trying to make contact with previously unknown tradespeople, making an extensive search, updating its lists, and offering a supportive or encouraging environment for new firms. This might be motivated by the desire to increase the share of bids or of contracts that would involve local firms or black run firms; perhaps better to reflect the composition of the population in the areas where the association is working. Our study suggested that in practice many associations are passive rather than active, with few making an energetic search and linking this with offering advice and support on a regular basis. Some associations had been prepared to vary or waive formal requirements for entry to approved lists of contractors, and there were occasional examples of negotiated rather than tendered contracts, and of nomination of subcontractors. It was possible to find innovative arrangements with white run contractor companies which not only included training but also help in the development of black run subcontracting firms. These things, however, tended to be very much the exception to the rule. Some officers suggested that it would not normally be possible to depart from usual tendering practices or to interfere in the choice of subcontractors without incurring unacceptable financial risks. On the whole - although we were studying associations with records of relatively good practice in the 'race' sphere - our case study housing associations had not developed proactive approaches to the employment of minority ethnic firms.

To illustrate their corporate commitment to the field of employment and training, seven associations cited involvement in 'local labour' initiatives. There is quite an extensive record in the housing association movement of connections with such initiatives, which may sometimes involve a main contractor undertaking to use labour drawn from specific localities. Although clearly a proactive type of operation, this has often required funding from outside mainstream housing investment, and will not automatically lead to greater use of black run firms on regular contract work. An emphasis on special ad hoc initiatives of this type may temporarily improve opportunities for work experience and training for local people, but should not deflect attention from access to ordinary contracts on a day to day basis.

The employment of minority ethnic contractors

Few housing associations adequately monitor and review their use of contractors. Out of the twenty associations studied, only three appeared to have reasonably systematic and fully operational systems for monitoring the flow of work to individual black run firms, for keeping the use of contractors under review, and for reporting regularly on these matters to committee. In a fourth case an association was capable of doing these things, but until very recently had had no minority ethnic contractors on its approved lists. Most of the associations had not prioritized the black contractors issue. Sometimes a commitment to considering black run firms depended on an individual active housing association officer, so that a personnel change might undermine progress. Were that particular officer to leave or change post, momentum would be lost. Such people are sometimes best seen - borrowing Bayo Fasheitan's description - as 'equal opportunities champions', who try to keep key issues on the agenda. On the other hand, in some associations at least, there were clear indications of a strong and definite corporate commitment, going beyond one or two specific active individuals. Clearly, an effective set of monitoring and reporting procedures would have been one form of evidence that an association was committed as an organization to good practice in the contractors field. Unfortunately, given the poor quality of monitoring in many cases, it was sometimes difficult to measure the share of contracts by value going to minority ethnic firms; while data covering subcontractors or on-site staffing had rarely been collected at all by associations. Nonetheless, our study was able to reach some reliable conclusions about the overall patterns in the use of minority ethnic firms and tradespeople.

There was wide variation in the links with black run and minority ethnic contractors, some associations having several on their approved lists of firms and making use of them, while some other associations had hardly any. Large contracts for development work had very rarely been awarded to black run firms, although there were a few exceptions (mainly in London and Birmingham). There were twelve associations for which the research obtained precise numbers of black run firms on approved development lists: half of these had only one black run firm on their list or none at all. Two other associations for which there was reasonable information (apart from the twelve) also appeared to have no black run contractors in development. This may be compared with the total numbers where known of firms (white and black run) on approved development lists, which ranged from 12 to 200, the majority of associations listing between 15 and 65. For repair and maintenance contracts the known numbers of black run firms on approved lists varied between none and seven, with the exception of one association which had 27. Most associations had made use of less than five black run firms in maintenance and repair work during the last twelve months. The main exception was the association with 27 approved black run maintenance and repair contractors, which had spent 90% of its budget via these firms. This was a black run London based association which had a reputation as a leader in this field. The approved lists held by associations in most cases included between 12 and 50 firms for repairs/maintenance work, and black run firms usually made up only a small percentage of the list. In some instances no contracts at all had been awarded to these minority ethnic firms in the previous year. Across the country the setting of targets for channelling proportions of contracted work to black run firms was rare. The overall impression from housing associations - with a few notable exceptions - was that *only a small share of construction investment and related expenditure was finding its way to minority ethnic firms.*

In one of the northern cities where case studies were pursued, the research evaluated performance within a group of associations and in the local freestanding care and repair scheme, as well as establishing contact with a variety of other local organizations. This meant we were able to obtain a good indication of the use made across the city of minority ethnic contractors, and of the local building industry scene. Despite strong awareness of the significance of the issue, associations' use of black led contractors was very limited, and this was so even in the area of maintenance and repairs. Those firms that were on approved lists here were mostly small, and predominantly specialist. The care and repair scheme, however, had allocated a larger share of its work to minority ethnic firms than had the associations. This might have reflected partly the type of work available in care and repair at a time when rehabilitation expenditure by associations was not at a high level. Inner city work of this kind may be attractive for black run firms, particularly where they wish to move beyond (or have already moved beyond) being one or two person operations. At the same time the care and repair scheme had had a much shorter history than most of the associations, and therefore perhaps less of an established communications network or set of customary practices linking it with particular white run firms. The scheme also had a large number of minority ethnic clients, many of whom might have been expected to welcome a builder with appropriate language skills apart from English.

The contractors and their experiences

Case study work and other information suggested that many black run firms were small, often operating at a level of one person or a small group of tradespeople, and often specialized. Some of our case study firms were inexperienced in housing association or local authority work, and might know little about associations or their requirements. Nonetheless, in some places there were larger companies, occasionally capable of taking on or participating in major schemes. Possibilities of developing consortia were also being pursued in some parts of the country as a means of overcoming the limitations of capacity and competitiveness of small firms. There was also some evidence of networks whereby firms or tradespeople worked with or subcontracted for each other. Although we were not able to explore gender issues in any depth, there did seem to be some networking developing amongst women contractors and tradespeople (black and white). On the other hand we did not encounter much evidence that large white run firms subcontracted to minority ethnic tradespeople on housing association contracts.

Minority ethnic contractors can experience a range of difficulties, including a mismatch between their preferences and the types of work on offer, difficulties in dealing with housing association requirements for entry to approved lists, and problems with the tendering process. The issue of pricing for tendering purposes can be important. Inexperience and lack of information may mean that a firm prices too high, and this can be made more likely if the proprietor is approaching the job in an ad hoc way. A well established firm with easier finances, supplies and credit, familiar with housing associations, and dealing with a number of similar contracts, may be able to undercut the newcomer. The 'costs of entry' for the small black run firm can include dealing with unaccustomed paperwork, learning about the association's requirements, meeting criteria to do with insurance or financial risk, and demonstrating capacity clearly. Once a firm is on an approved list, however, there is no guarantee of a flow of work, or even of invitations to tender. Even so, some minority ethnic firms have managed to obtain contracts from more than one housing association. Where a firm is successful in securing a number of jobs from more than one association, that firm's availability and reliability might mean that local housing associations do not try so hard to find other black run firms for their approved lists. In effect there can be some danger of tokenism if associations are content to draw from a narrow pool, having satisfied any internal or external political pressures to 'find some black contractors'.

Initiatives, innovations and improved practices

This can be considered at the level of housing associations acting individually, or in terms of joint initiatives such as the creation and operation of trades registers or directories. At the individual level a number of associations have tried to recruit minority ethnic contractors and tradespeople on a proactive basis. Actions can range from officers using discretionary authority in commissioning small scale repairs, to waiving some of the formal requirements of entry to approved lists, or giving firms a trial on a probationary basis, offering technical guidance, or the possibility of a negotiated contract. The local environment seems to be a factor facilitating or making difficult proactive efforts: if few black led firms are known among housing association staff, and if the network of business contacts is poor, then recruitment may seem uphill work. The absence of a comprehensive up to date register of firms (or of any register of firms) can be significant here. Developing a network of valued and reliable contacts may not be straightforward for some associations. Even a keen officer with modest targets may fail to make progress - given constraints of time and resources - if the local networks are underdeveloped. This might imply that in the absence of a register some coordinated action between housing associations might be more successful and more easily sustained than an independent initiative. By contrast, some black run associations are able - or ought to be able - to mobilize their community connections in order to find appropriate firms. Here there might be scope in the long term for acting as a channel of information for white run associations. At present, however, some minority ethnic associations are still too dependent on larger white run partners or former development agents to have a pool of black run firms or the capacity to channel much work to them. The advent of large scale consortia, involving several associations developing a scheme, can also have an impact here. Where a small black run association is one of the participants, it may be able to exert relatively little influence over the distribution of contracts. It should be noted, furthermore, that a small association may feel it is in a weaker position to take risks than a larger one; therefore using an established contractor with a strong track record may be attractive even if that firm is white run. Despite these obstacles, some of the minority ethnic associations have demonstrated that more work can be channelled to black contractors, if the will exists to do so.

Once contractors have been admitted to approved lists - and often beforehand too - there are possibilities for systematically encouraging and assisting them. Given the problems they can have with pricing, estimating, etc., there is considerable scope for developments in training, although not necessarily always via individual associations. At the level of internal practices, associations can begin by tightening up their monitoring and review processes. Any association committed to equal opportunities should expect to be able to report to committee regularly on the distribution of work by value among firms, taking note of ethnic origin (and disability and gender). Such an association would need to have procedures in place for recording and analysing the information, and probably an annual review process to check on the composition of the approved lists and the changing capacity of firms. This might mean some regular discussions with contractors about capacity, flow of work, etc. Ideally there ought to be some means for also knowing about the levels of work going to black subcontractors. Once there is a reasonable system for monitoring and review, targeting becomes more feasible. This is a way of trying to improve the distribution of tendering opportunities or commissioned jobs, so that black run firms are less excluded. Individual associations might wish to set targets for the percentages of work to go to black run or local firms, or to firms on a local register. This type of approach is not very common at present but has the merit of being a definite corporate commitment against which achievements can be measured. Targeting in relation to a comprehensive register would also give associations an incentive to offer support and advice to firms on that register; both in terms of getting them onto approved lists and in terms of contract bidding, advice on pricing, etc.

Registered firms themselves might need to have some performance targets on finance, tendering skills or management which they would work towards in cooperation with trainers and associations. Additionally, targeting by associations could make their officers more careful to match offered jobs to capacity of firms, and perhaps more likely to break down some jobs into more manageable components to fit the skills of local contractors. At a very practical level associations could consider some of their detailed procedures; in particular ensuring prompt payment, and where possible interim/staged payments. An active association might also wish to consider the advantages and disadvantages of possible strategies like rotation of tender opportunities to contractors on approved maintenance lists.

Turning now to joint actions, we need to focus in particular on registers or directories of minority ethnic firms and trades. This has been seen as a way of improving the information housing associations have about contractors, and enlarging the chances firms have of being taken seriously. Such registers may also cover firms run by disabled people or by women, or may cover all firms from a specified local area. In Birmingham and London efforts have been made to set up registers so that prospective clients can draw on these when commissioning work. The two key initiatives supported by housing associations and relevant to black run firms in these cities have been the Birmingham Inner City Builders Support Unit (BICBUS) and the London Equal Opportunities Federation (LEOF). In London the Black Contractors Association (BCA) has also maintained its own members' register, and has offered training and support to firms. There have been other attempts to create registers, sometimes under Task Force auspices, but none has yet been as significant for black people as BICBUS, LEOF and the BCA. We understand that another register is being established in Lancashire, and others may follow elsewhere, inspired by the London and Birmingham models. Related specifically to the gender dimension there is also a London based organization which in some ways parallels LEOF or the BCA; this is Women and Manual Trades (WAMT).

Provided a register is kept up to date and reflects the full range of local firms, then its existence makes it harder for associations to argue that they cannot find appropriate black run contractors. The creation of a register may also heighten awareness of the issues amongst associations, and alert contractors to opportunities in the social housing sector. From our case study work, however, it appears that there can also be some limitations. A place on a register does not guarantee that a contractor will be accepted onto any approved list or be invited to tender. Nor will entry to the register necessarily represent a sufficient guarantee of quality or capacity from the point of view of any individual association. On the other hand, membership of a register cannot be seen as an absolute prerequisite of applying for work, since for a variety of reasons some firms do not join. There seems to be a mixed experience of the value of registers, so that they are probably best seen as a successful first step which can be built on, rather than an adequate and complete solution. There are initiatives which link entry to a register with access to training and support, and there is also the possibility of registered firms trying to overcome the disadvantages of small size by combining their resources. Going further, the concept of formally establishing locally based consortia of black led firms (already noted above) appears to offer some advantages, but it is too early to judge whether such consortia will prove worthwhile or lasting. A group of firms that are members of a register can provide a basis for such a consortium.

We have run through some of the potential ways forward for giving black run firms a fairer chance of entry and success in housing association work, but there are powerful *limiting factors*. Neither improved internal housing association practices, nor training initiatives or proactive efforts by individual associations, can alter the current financial climate within which contracts are awarded, or compensate fully for the disadvantages any weakly resourced firms face by contrast with larger or strongly established competitors. Trends towards design and build contracts, 'off the shelf' purchase of completed housing by associations, narrowly defined value for money criteria, and shifts in the pattern of investment in schemes, may all militate against enlarging the share of work going to minority ethnic firms. In many contexts large established companies are bound to be at an advantage.

Even when schemes are dominated by very large firms, however, there may be some possibility for looking at nomination of subcontractors. In any event, no financial considerations should preclude requiring main contractors and consultants to demonstrate active awareness of equal opportunities issues, nor can it excuse an association from the need to educate as well as monitor main contractors. Going further, even in today's financial climate there may be opportunities for a main white run contractor to agree innovative provisions which benefit minority ethnic business development. In one unusual instance covered in our case studies, arrangements for actions by a large firm on a big housing association contract included helping set up a black run painters and decorators by a start-up loan (with this new firm to be used on the development), subcontracting carpet laying to a local black run firm, creating six trainee posts, using a black run security firm to patrol the site, and improving the main contractor's own equal opportunities training, etc. (see Harrison and Davies, 1995).

Summary and conclusions

Our research has indicated that only a small share of the economic benefits arising from housing association urban investment is finding its way to minority ethnic communities in the form of building work commissioned from black run firms. This means that the main indirect beneficiaries of this type of inner city investment are white run firms. The same pattern (or an even more marked one) would probably be found in the fields of office services and purchase of supplies, and for consultancy services, although we did not gather systematic data on these. The pattern amounts to a situation of indirect negative discrimination, an extraordinary outcome in an area of expenditure which is supposed to assist inner city residents. Central government can be seen to be securing very poor 'value for money' indeed, if we take into account the potential impact of such investment on local urban regeneration. There are steps that housing associations could take to improve their monitoring, their local communications and their recruitment practices, and this might have some impact. At the same time more availability of training support might help. The development of registers is also something which can benefit black run firms. None of these positive advances, however, would change the general financial environment or the broad pattern of resources and criteria which determine who gains most from involvement in public investment capital works. Minority ethnic communities would still be likely to continue to lose out in the distribution of gains.

In earlier chapters we located some of the causative factors leading to this kind of outcome, which is probably not untypical of urban policy in general in the UK. In a different political environment it might have been possible to use the indirect impact of urban public investment deliberately as a way of reducing inequalities in resources and opportunities, and assisting economic development in black communities. This could have run counter, however, to economic liberal views about competition, and to paternalistic centralizing ideas about controlling the way expenditures are made (see chapter 3). If genuine community empowerment had been an objective of policies, then local people would have had the opportunity for a say on who should gain from contracts, how they should be awarded, and what indirect benefits should be sought from them for the locality and its people. The slogan of free competition could not have been used so easily to oppose contract compliance measures.

Perhaps, however, there are ways of resolving some of the tensions between economic liberalism and local participation. For instance, one option could be to recast official conceptions of value for money so that community regeneration could be taken account of more explicitly and systematically. Thus competition would remain open, but tenders would have to demonstrate what local indirect gains there might be. Such an approach would give large white run companies

123

an incentive to consider employing local people and subcontracting firms, and also give locally based small building firms a chance of overcoming the entry barriers that at present in effect prevent them from competing on an equal basis. It might stimulate the development of local suppliers too, since local purchasing might be one way of evidencing community regeneration gains. Such a way forward would also avoid the hidden danger that enforcing economic liberalism's ideas in disadvantaged communities could have. For resistance to the award of contracts to outsiders via 'free' competition could potentially manifest itself in various forms of active legal and illegal opposition and obstruction, and in the 'corruption' of decision making processes by private informal deals to make sure that local firms get a 'rake off'. We have not found any evidence at all of these things in our case studies, but there are a few anecdotes already which might point the way towards an unpleasant future. It would be an unfortunate consequence of present government notions of value for money if it became impossible for white workers or managers to be on site without physical protection.

Notes

1. The NFHA and other housing organizations also took an interest at this time; see Voluntary Housing, April 1989. More recently, see Salami, 1991.
2. Results from this large programme are being published by the Joseph Rowntree Foundation, and will also be brought together in a forthcoming book edited by Michael Ball. Amongst the other specific Rowntree studies within the programme was a very successful Glasgow University project looking at 15 initiatives targeting construction expenditure on disadvantaged localities; this in some respects parallels our project.

7 Movements, politics and empowerment

It is now time to bring together some of our more general concerns about political relationships, relating these to empirical material referred to in chapters 4, 5 and 6. We will try to summarize features or issues that seem significant in understanding the welfare state and struggles within it.

Firstly, this chapter will suggest that analyses of the politics of 'black housing issues' - while specific - might be linked with a general overview of strategies, new social welfare movements, and mobilizations over empowerment. The key theme here will be that interaction with state agencies can be crucial in a situation where 'the state' is heavily involved in the management of consumption by households. Thus, while pressures from the grass roots help shape public policies, there can be scope for a degree of incorporation, with the activities of state agencies influencing the directions and forms of collective social action.

Secondly, as we have demonstrated in earlier chapters, externally set limits inherent in firmly established characteristics of the welfare state may restrict collective empowerment and what it can achieve for communities and groups, as well as inhibiting the strategies that individual households can adopt. Efforts to ameliorate or offset the deterioration of inner cities have to be understood alongside the characteristics of a welfare state which regularly empowers and disempowers people in differentiating ways; through laws, mainstream spending programmes, taxation policies, etc. Explicit urban policies have done little to change underlying socioeconomic forces or patterns, but have in any case been directly constrained by longstanding features of UK social policy. The constraints on empowerment for poor communities lie in the predispositions of economic liberalism, in public expenditure limits, in the tensions between centralism, paternalism and localism in what is a highly centralized polity, in a reluctance to accept diversity of aspirations, and in the tensions between individual and collective modes of decision making. At the same time we must be aware of the precarious nature of assistance founded on principles of selectivity within a complex welfare state, a precariousness that may be exacerbated at times of economic recession. We also note the significance of property in relation to mobilization and empowerment. Relationships with state agencies may open channels of access to property rights and allied resources in ways that help determine how far empowerment becomes meaningful for groups as well as individuals. Without control of resources, people remain relatively powerless.

Thirdly, the implications of separatism, localism or particularism must be reviewed, alongside a consideration of individual rights. Separatism need not always prove beneficial for households. A separate channel of provision may present problems to those it aims to help, as well as opening up opportunities for them. There is also scope for exclusiveness, negative discrimination, and abuse of power; particularly when an organization or group restricts who may have access to resources. If policy makers wish to protect individuals, then this points towards some kind of universalism, a topic to which we will return in our final chapter.

The state, incorporation, and social welfare movements

Many grass roots organizations confront those of the state, or align themselves in relation to public policies; thus interactions with official agencies are often crucial. Although the empirical material in earlier chapters relates primarily to 'race', there are plenty of parallels in other contexts. A great deal has been written on collective mobilizations and direct action, and there are growing literatures on self organization and social movements amongst women, older people and disabled people. We cannot review the literature here, but will briefly comment on parallels in an area that has too often been disregarded. Oliver and Zarb discuss the disability movement as a new social movement, noting amongst other features the increasing numbers of centres for independent and integrated living established in several countries as both 'an attempt to achieve self-actualisation, and a form of direct action aimed at creating new solutions to problems defined by disabled people themselves' (1989,p.230). They also note - as we have done in earlier chapters - the issue of incorporation, and the political and strategy choices this raises for participants in movements and struggles (see p.235). Pursuing some related themes on disability and direct action, Shakespeare points to the importance of 'developing parallels with other social movements' (1993, p.252), and discusses the politics and issues of identity. He argues that historically black people and women have been disenfranchised, and that this has applied to disabled people too, who have faced obstacles to registration and voting, let alone effective political participation. His comments

126

highlight the potentially empowering role of direct action (see p.253). He also points out that in the sociological literature on new social movements, 'none of the major theorists mention disability' (p.257). In common with the present study, Shakespeare appears concerned to indicate that struggles may be about resource allocation and the establishing of citizenship rights:

> The movements of women, black people and disabled people have shown that these constituencies have not benefited from the post-war developments in both living standards and social rights, and demonstrated the continuing inequalities in access to both political and economic power (see pp.258-9).

Battles over material circumstances or cultural exclusion can often be bound up closely with patterns of political disadvantage and lack of social rights. For, as Edwards puts it, marginalisation implies 'society's failure to keep all its population within the embrace of participative citizenship' (1989,p.12).

It would be possible to cite other writers who have considered social movements in ways that connect with our own analysis. At the outset, however, we have directed attention to social welfare movements rather than social movements in general, and the struggle for a satisfactory place within the state management of consumption has been our primary focus. Thus our analysis is in one sense narrower than that found in some of the work on new social movements, and is likely to find its closest parallels in studies of mobilizations over legislation, funding and the structure of services provision in social policy areas. As chapter 6 made clear, however, there are strong links between consumption provision and employment generation. In a sense, housing 'intervention' by state agencies is multi-faceted in its effects, so that housing can be seen as a 'total experience' for communities rather than being treated in compartmentalized policy categories.[1] Grass roots activists will not necessarily think in the same terms as policy makers, and may combine employment, environmental, social services, cultural and housing concerns. We cannot define the purposes or scope of any social movement without looking closely at its history, commitments and experiences. In other words, whatever informative parallels we may find, we must recognise diversity of purpose and character, and in emphasizing consumption we must also remain aware of other dimensions of state activity which interest activists. Even so, diverse movements may share some common relationships with the apparatus of the state, and face some similar limits to empowerment.

It is feasible to generalize to some extent from our material on the black voluntary housing movement, while bearing in mind the specific nature of events. Where marginalised groups secure footholds in the public policy arena they are likely to be influenced in a number of ways by interactions with state agencies and other powerful actors. As chapter 5 showed, group characteristics, form, and definition of immediate purpose may be influenced by the stance of bodies which offer finance and other resources. This influence may extend to the composition of committees in a new organization, to the relationships with larger potential partners or allies, and to the priority given to specific schemes and ways of moving forward. Our case studies show that the sponsorship of the Housing Corporation (and other organizations) became crucial to the chances groups had of developing their own viable housing organizations and - later - making them grow towards independence. Inevitably, therefore, they responded to the funding priorities and plans of the Corporation, while at the same time exerting an influence on these plans. It seems likely that in some other public policy spheres a similar two way process can operate, whereby a group or movement feeds in significant ideas, knowledge and demands, but also finds its activities and direction shaped to some extent by official purposes and priorities. In any event, the process of incorporation is a well recognised phenomenon, which may affect interest and pressure groups, corporate organizations, and professions, as well as broader movements. Relationships between state agencies and powerful outside interests may be partly a matter of convergence and mutual accommodation, but the state's 'clients' among black communities will tend to be small scale bodies with far less leverage. Where there is an element of tokenism on the part of an official agency, or where resources are tightly restricted, there can be a strong element of dependency on the part of small black run organizations, with ever present fears of being 'funded for failure'.

We can add to this a more general interpretation about the development of the welfare state itself, and its relationships with constituencies and interests. The welfare state is (amongst other things) an ensemble of modes of intermediation, representation and 'intervention', shifting over time. As it develops its array of forms of support and systems of consumption management, that development not only reflects politics but also affects the scope for political mobilization and representation, and invites further struggles over resources. In our example the ground for mobilization was to some extent created or shaped by legislation, state agencies, and the pre-existing pattern of influence, politics and beneficiaries. In other words the social movement did not grow in a vacuum, but emerged in a specific context against a backcloth of unequal resource distribution, racism, institutional power, and areas of opportunity for change. The implication is that collective action can be intimately tied in with the particular character of a specific welfare state; details are important.

The limits to empowerment

In earlier chapters we observed the severe limits over the extent to which community or locality level empowerment for marginalised groups could occur in UK cities. Some factors setting limits on the scope of government attempts to assist inner areas were cited in chapter 3. They included: the dominance of economic liberalism; economic decline allied with public expenditure constraints; the centralizing and paternalistic traditions of governmental social policy; the reluctance to accept diversity of aspirations, needs and cultures; and the reluctance to acknowledge the distributional impact of those public policies that were not focussed on marginalised groups. Later, in chapters 4, 5 and 6, we noted some of the concerns around the question of housing empowerment for minority ethnic communities in particular. Individual and collective strategies of black and minority ethnic households have had to develop in an environment permeated by racisms and economic disadvantage. Now we will confirm the connections between specific experiences 'in the field' and the general obstacles that set limits.

Economic liberalism exerts a powerful limiting effect, for it presupposes some commodification of mainstream services, 'free' competition, and individual consumer choice 'maximised' through markets rather than collective decision making. For some better off black households, markets may have opened doors to opportunity and improved conditions, but even here there have been disadvantages due to racism, 'risk avoidance' by suppliers or lenders, etc. (see chapter 4 for fuller comments). Furthermore, the empowerment of low income owner-occupiers through urban renewal policies has been very incomplete (see chapter 3), while few black households are likely to have benefited so far through assisted entry to ownership via special schemes (shared ownership, etc.).

More importantly for some poorer households, the political dominance of the philosophy of commodification and markets has been one reason for the tendency for social rented housing to be pushed in a safety net direction in the 1980s and early 1990s, with consumers being stigmatized more than before. Rather than being seen as a social right, rented housing becomes seen as a matter for markets, unless one is defined as a member of some 'special need' category. Welfare provision is seen as a 'gift' awarded subject to measures of relative need, and the terms of the gift may restrict the degree of control the recipient or group of recipients has over it or its capital value. Since the resources are conceived of as a gift rather than a right, the degree of empowerment in use of the funds can be limited. Indeed people seeking to benefit by obtaining homes may be subject to discipline or denial (as we noted in chapter 2). If the monies are to be channelled through an organization representing consumers, that organization or group may have to bid for funds within a very specific remit, where purposes are compartmentalized in ways which would not necessarily reflect the aspirations of participants. Collective participation in housing fits ill with economic liberalism, since it might imply local political interference with the management and purpose of the gift. There can be serious tensions between ideas about individualized modes of choosing on the one hand - with each person acting alone as consumer, purchaser or client - and collective participatory methods of managing resources. Anti-collectivist market ideologies have been reinforced by public expenditure constraints made more severe by governmental failures of economic management and growth. In this climate central government has reduced bricks and mortar subsidy, and encouraged commercialization, competitive tendering and more direct involvement of private capital. Local authority roles have been diminished while housing associations have been pressed in the direction of private capital markets and 'cost effective schemes'; implying prioritizing strong organizations with good asset bases in terms of owned stock, and perhaps reducing quality standards (see chapter 5). The choice of appropriate scheme development options has been influenced by simplistic notions of value for money which have inhibited inner city renewal projects that appear costly, and attempted to replicate private market criteria in the public housing domain. With small amounts of owned housing stock, and serving inner city constituencies where development options are likely to be expensive, black run housing associations may feel constrained or threatened by this developing environment. In some cases their position remains precarious, with a high degree of dependency on white run organizations. Prioritizing support for their development could be justified officially over the last decade partly by stressing the ad hoc, temporary and 'special' nature of the need. Once the Housing Corporation's second five year programme ends, the new black run associations may be expected to meet 'normal' criteria. This set of circumstances makes the genuine empowerment of minority ethnic communities through their own housing organizations difficult. Some of these organizations might be in danger of becoming 'white associations with black faces', moving in the same commercial direction as other housing associations, and perhaps even having to set higher rents than larger counterparts. It is difficult for them to empower their clients because of many factors beyond the organizations' control (see chapter 5).

The implications of economic liberalism carry through into the sphere of community regeneration too, as our findings in chapter 6 imply. The indirect benefits reaching minority ethnic communities through building work appear slight. Yet prioritizing the use of local firms or local labour would challenge some basic assumptions about competition. Although the reality in the building industry is nothing like a free market one, nonetheless there would be strong political resistance from vested interests to any 'contract compliance' or similar approach which sought to help local areas through assuring them a share in the earnings from housing investment.[2] For local people, however, no simple dividing line is necessarily drawn between their housing, employment or regeneration concerns. Returning to our comments above, we can say that the 'gift' of housing monies from the state is likely to be closely circumscribed here in a way that certainly can be out of line with local preferences and perceptions. This is not an issue confined to the inner cities. In rural Wales, as a parallel, perhaps we might expect hostility to the award of any building contracts to large non Welsh firms working for housing associations in districts where Welsh language and culture are issues of concern. There is a history of debate over the occupancy of homes in Welsh speaking areas anyway, since the 'free market' brings in second home owners and other outsiders who may undermine the continuance of traditional culture. The tension between economic liberalism and localism is clear here just as it is in the inner urban context. If localism meant establishing a dual housing market (with some houses reserved for locals), or a dual contracts market (with some contracts always awarded locally), then it would be likely to be unacceptable for economic liberals.

Turning to paternalism, centralization and reluctance to accept diversity, we can observe a number of outcomes in our specific field. Despite development of consultation with black run organizations (alongside mainstream white run ones) the dominant housing policy voices are still those of central government Conservative politicians and the treasury. The national Conservative Party agenda remains crucial in shaping the degree and nature of financial support, and the extent of empowerment which is feasible. So although government ministers accepted the Housing Corporation's five year programmes, these programmes were always likely to become marginalised if out of line with more fundamental objectives. In the late 1980s, as strategies for restructuring social rented housing developed, black run associations remained an acceptable part (for ministers) of an overall package for growth in the voluntary sector's role. On the other hand, they could easily be undermined by the movement of the financial climate in a more commercial direction. Given the concentration of power at the centre, central government could take an overall ideological and financial path which disregarded minority interests. In effect the post-1988 housing association environment did threaten to marginalise the new black run associations. As we have already noted, the underlying thrust was influenced by faith in markets and private capital, and crude concepts of value for money. Despite political pressure from housing organizations, and awareness within the Housing Corporation of weaknesses of the new regimes in terms of adverse consequences, government pressed on. The reason why economic liberal ideology and monetarism can have such a strong influence on housing policy is partly because central government has so much power in its hands as far as social policies are concerned. We commented on this, and on the undemocratic characteristics of urban policies, in earlier chapters. Ministers can set out the legislative framework taking very little notice of objections, even in a field like homelessness with previously a measure of cross-party and practice agency consensus on policy (see for instance Carter and Ginsburg, 1994). These characteristics of UK government mean that, despite talk of pluralism, collective participation is often uphill work. If government does support a new service or acknowledge an interest, this may be done in a tokenistic or paternalistic spirit, and create relationships of dependency. The vulnerability of some minority ethnic housing associations - as of some other black people's organizations - owes much to the fact that central government need pay little regard to sources of ideas outside the governing party. At the same time, government neither needs nor wishes to acknowledge any adverse distributional affects that its policies in other fields (employment, transport, social security, education, wealth, etc.) may be having on marginalised communities. To some degree the conditions of the inner cities or on difficult housing estates are presented in social pathology terms by Conservatives. They are less likely to be discussed as an aspect of shifting socioeconomic inequalities and differences in power. So any form of substantial aid will be given cautiously, and under controlled conditions, so as not to encourage further 'deviance' or a 'dependency culture' (Coleman, 1991, contains good examples of the type of thinking involved). Partly because of this ideological orientation, support will never match what has been given through other channels of the social division of welfare; the response to black people's demands will be muted.

This is not a simple or static situation, however, and there are examples of successes for black people which suggest that governmental agencies are sometimes open to pressure or persuasion; to an extent the Housing Corporation has been an example of this. There has also been effective opposition to specific policies such as Housing Action Trusts, which were resisted by (white and black) council tenants in several places. Furthermore, some UK governmental bodies do appear more receptive to cultural diversity than was once the case. They are not necessarily able to transfer much power to communities at the local level, though, since financial regimes and programme goals are set centrally with a strong political party input. Even in Wales and Scotland, where Conservatives cannot claim any kind of mandate in terms of electoral support, central government has pressed forward with unpopular ideas; some people have argued that Scotland has even been used as a quasi-colonial laboratory in which to test certain policies prior to applying them in England.

Two additional points need to be made about the limits on empowerment in UK social policy. Given the importance of economic liberal perceptions and the strength of groups that are already well catered for through politics, the most likely model for assisting marginalised groups and individuals is a selectivist one. Assistance will not only be defined as a gift, but will be confined to the identifiably needy and will be subject to periodic assessment, review, challenge and reappraisal. For social rented housing, challenges can range from regular policing of housing organizations in order to ensure that they perform 'adequately', to occasional racist-inspired attacks on the type of people being housed (see chapter 5, note 9). As we asserted earlier in this book, selectivism serving the relatively poor tends to be precarious. It is vulnerable to expenditure cuts or to political attacks from those who perceive that 'their taxes' are maintaining the undeserving. In the case of social rented housing there have been frequent attempts since the 1970s to curtail expenditure and to encourage more market orientated alternatives. This sets limits on the degree of genuine empowerment that can be hoped for through social rented tenure, since tenant empowerment requires some politically secure claims over resource allocation. Recent cuts in housing association programmes - and the emphasis on encouraging ownership or shared ownership - reflect the lack of political influence of potential tenants and those who voice their needs.

This leads us into the issue of property rights. Minority ethnic housing organizations have been well aware that empowerment and security connect with control of property and resources. In present day Britain that means owning the housing stock with as full legal title as possible, unencumbered by heavy financial or other obligations except to the client community. What often applies to individuals and their strategies, in this respect, can also apply to organizations. The financial independence which would make black run associations less vulnerable in the long term is tied up with owning the stock without excessive debts, rather than being mere management agents for a larger partner association. The general principle here is that lasting empowerment often requires a substantial share in property rights, either directly as an individual or indirectly through organizations in which one has a sense of voice and ownership. This is because such rights have become key building blocks for the welfare state in Western countries like the UK, as we indicated in earlier chapters. Selectivist programmes can sometimes provide routes into ownership and control, but in the case of minority ethnic housing associations this has been a slow track and a tortuous one to travel.

None of this implies that systems of welfare built around property rights for groups or individuals are unproblematic. Ownership usually embodies powers to exclude non-owners and to transfer rights over capital or accommodation to subsequent occupiers. For instance, tenants with a strong sense of 'ownership' in a housing scheme might hope to be able to hand on their tenancies to sons and daughters. Clearly, limits may be set by funding agencies over the extent of local power of this kind, in the interests of equality of status of other potential applicants, or in order to avoid corruption.

Implications of separatism, pluralism, and particularism; the strengths of individualism and the market

Although we have noted tensions between economic liberalism and individualism on the one hand, and localism and collectivism on the other, the arguments so far have focussed more on the collective than on the strengths of individualism or the politics of individual social rights. It is necessary to restore the balance.

The case for individualism

From a historical perspective, modern individualistic ideas need to be understood by contrasting them with feudal or religious power as well as by relating them to the development of capitalistic economic arrangements. The notion of the abstract individual with rights provided a counterweight to claims for hegemony by autocratic rulers, and to the rigidities of persons each having a predetermined place assigned through status or caste. As a substitute for feudal power or socialist management, the market builds on this idea of the individual through concepts of choice. In a democratic environment individuals can apparently pursue their interests without having to hammer out a mutually agreed definition of the public good or the best way forward. Reconciling supply and expressed demand, markets allocate resources and draw in investments in ways that appear to make unnecessary the imposition of an overall plan. So the market offers a type of 'right' which seems orientated to individual choice.

Unfortunately, for minority ethnic households, market relationships have not been very empowering. Household strategies have been circumscribed by relative poverty, racist treatment from intermediaries, and other disadvantages (see chapter 4). While individual paths have led some to obtain secure and high quality assets, this has been the exception rather than the norm. The inadequacy of markets does not necessarily mean, however, that individualized strategies or some aspects of market relationships will always be ineffective or unproductive for marginalised consumers. Markets can be regulated, while individualized solutions may be pursued or protected through collective organization (as potentially in the case of shared ownership). One test of any arrangement here might be to measure the extent that poorer people felt empowered by it, and more able to sustain or evolve their own strategies.

Of course, individualism need not rely only on markets, but can depend on a variety of ideas about 'social' rights, including rights to welfare outside markets (as well as equal treatment within them). This confers a different kind of freedom or security. Individually distributed justiciable or customary rights can protect areas of daily life from the intrusions of politicians or bureaucrats, reducing costs of engaging in political interactions. Some scholars, however, interpret the 'costs' of engaging in politics as a benefit, believing that involvement in civil society is itself developmental, and leads to better information and mutual accommodation. Nonetheless, the rights claims of individuals should not be overlooked in any discussion of the merits of collective organization.

These concerns are directly relevant in the housing field we have been looking at, since collective organization has been taking place along somewhat separatist and localist lines, and this could conceivably cut against certain ideas about individuals, their opportunities and rights.

Particularism and its consequences in housing

In an incisive paper Spicker (1993/94) has set out some of the implications of what is described as particularism, and has linked this with communitarianism. Particularism refers to the idea that different standards should be applied to different people, a notion derived from longstanding traditions in culture and politics. It may imply a presumption in favour of certain discriminatory structures. By contrast with universalism, which can imply that the same rules are applied to everyone, particularism can lead to prioritizing the needs or standing of specific groups according to some criteria of exclusion and inclusion. Spicker comments that communitarianism can be taken to stand for a 'highly socialised view of people in which their moral position can be understood only in terms of their social relationships'. He asserts that communitarian critiques challenge the basis on which judgements about society can be made, and 'imply that different standards will be applied in different places' (p.7). Thus there is a 'debate between universalism and communitarianism' which cuts across the conventional political divisions of left and right. For present purposes the central themes are that from a communitarian or particularist perspective differences between people should lead to diverse responses, but that we should be aware that this can be both positive and negative in its values and impact. Where a welfare system is genuinely pluralistic it may be concerned to accommodate local, cultural or other solidarities, and to channel resources in ways which reflect this. Reinforcing or accommodating difference, or applying different rules in differing socioeconomic settings, however, is not without potentially adverse consequences. If UK social policies were to be focussed more often through locality or community, and to confer higher levels of empowerment, this might disadvantage groups who were left out or who refused to accept the ruling values in their 'community'. As Spicker puts it, the 'emphasis on diversity is difficult to reconcile with the norms usually associated with universal principles of distribution, like minimum guarantees or optimal provision' (p.15). While the communitarian's arguments may refer to 'social networks, mutual aid and collective action', at the same time 'some aspects of particularism are repellent;

the idea can be used to justify racism, inequality, patronage and injustice' (p.16). Indeed, the formal slogan of preserving or fostering a sense of community can serve to exclude outsiders in UK housing (for discussion of a relevant instance see Dalton and Daghlian, 1989,p.70). In the USA the motive of 'preservation of race or class exclusivity' could lead to 'most communities' resisting 'low or moderate income housing'; zoning laws could be invoked to prevent or restrict building schemes (McKay, 1977,p.125).

Looking further at housing we can see that a black run housing association - just like a white run one - might favour particular clients at the expense of others,[3] might be male dominated, and might have specific cultural leanings which made it unattractive to some potential tenants. This might preclude certain people from obtaining access to its dwellings or from serving on its management committee. Alternatively, in a situation of limited choice a tenant might wish to object if he or she were to be stereotyped as a 'suitable' client for a minority ethnic association simply because of ethnic origin, without regard to preference. In chapter 5 we discussed the empowerment of tenants, referring to ideas about participation and control, but this does not imply unproblematic solutions to questions of particularism, individual choice, and access. Tenants may not be unified or universally active, and may not take a friendly view of households unlike their own. Tenants' movements might fragment estate populations as well as unite them, or might be 'fractured by disagreements and conflicts of interest' (Cairncross, Clapham and Goodlad, 1993,p.179). They might try to exclude some kinds of households from an area, and 'race' or culture could be factors here. Given these realities we need to keep the rights of individual potential tenants in sight, both from the point of view of their expressing differences, and as a counterweight to the potentially oppressive and exclusive nature of some collective groupings. It is also likely that where there is a belief in shared material interests, this need not mean that tenants undervalue the importance of individual strategies.

In the field of building work a communitarian argument might suggest allocating contracts in ways that would benefit local firms or workers, or tradespeople with specific community connections. Yet this would accord an inferior status to other firms or individuals who might be precluded from bidding for such work. Were such an approach applied to an area occupied by traditional white working class households, then black run firms based elsewhere might lose out through the empowerment of local white people. Or, similarly, it might be viewed as alarming if an Asian builder was unable to bid for work in an area where Jewish, Irish or African/Caribbean households predominated.

In practice, discrimination in tenancy allocation and in awards of contract would be likely to be judged improper or illegal in the UK, and in both activities housing organizations may refer to externally determined codes or advice. Yet

136

the principle of prioritizing a specific group for benefits remains highly significant. One strong argument for positively discriminating in favour of non white minority ethnic households and their organizations is that black people are presently excluded and disadvantaged in many areas of experience. Consequently they may feel the need to pursue separatist and particularist strategies which should receive assistance. This need not presuppose that they do so without limitations or rules, and it is the relationship with general rules and policies to which we turn in our final chapter. The central political questions concern the relationships between individual rights and local or community power, and the balance between universalism and separatism.

Notes

1. The present writer has been influenced here by Michael Ball's observations during a meeting of researchers considering results from the Rowntree Foundation initiative on the construction industry.
2. See Edwards, 1989, pp.20-21, for some relevant 1980s history; see also Haughton, 1990,p.192, and Jesson, 1990.
3. In fact minority ethnic associations do not necessarily house black people only, and indeed could sometimes be subject to external pressures to take large numbers of white tenants; see Soares, 1993.

8 Conclusions: Reconstructing the welfare state?

During the last two decades there has been much discussion about changes in the character of the UK welfare state. Pluralism has moved up the agenda of policy makers and politicians, in an environment where the direct universalistic provision of services by state agencies has come under political attack. Parts of this book have been about state institutions accommodating or responding to a specific kind of pluralism, one based in a diversity of 'grass roots' cultures and attitudes, and fuelled by previous experiences of racism, as well as social, political and economic exclusion. The needs and expectations of minority ethnic groups are increasingly important in a number of western societies, and generate pressures for varying institutional responses and greater cultural sensitivity. At the same time racist discourses and practices are being challenged through a variety of strategies, sometimes particularistic and sometimes universalistic in their objectives.[1] Minority groups may often face a hard struggle to secure fairer treatment and a genuine place in the policy forum. Their daily experiences in housing - as we showed in chapter 4 - have included negative discrimination combined with economic disadvantage. Despite the obstacles, there have been many efforts to mobilize, in relation to a range of policy areas, with black people seeking roles in decision making and more access to resources. Our main focus has been on collective demands for empowerment of this kind in housing, on the capacity of agencies to respond, and on the scope and limitations of incorporation. We have also acknowledged the great variety of individual strategies pursued by households (and small businesses) to improve their positions, and we need to remember any connections these may have with collective efforts.

In earlier chapters we indicated a theoretical standpoint which saw welfare state structures partly as an ensemble of routes and mechanisms of consumption management and representation. The form and character of agency activities and responses within this structure are influenced by a variety of political and economic forces. Power and empowerment need to be understood in the context of the overall structures of welfare provision, and the constraints, and against the backcloth of legacies of racism, disablism and patriarchy. In chapter 3 we noted the limitations that have constrained the UK welfare state's responses to needy and marginalised groups in the specific context of urban policies. Although these policies might have been expected to help empower black people, the record is one of failure in this respect. Chapter 6 adds to the evidence. Nonetheless, there are signs of change, with our central case study - on the black voluntary housing movement - demonstrating something of a breakthrough in social policy.

In the sections below we will take up some concerns of principle that arise in relation to a changing welfare state. In particular, we will consider the implications pluralism of the kind we have discussed raises for the reconstruction of 'welfare' in the UK. We begin with a reminder of some of the broad options there might be for the future of welfare systems, drawing attention to rights based approaches and to particularistic ones related to groups and localities. Then the claims for groups and individuals will be considered. Finally the chapter will examine the possible reconciliation of strategies to meet collective and individual demands.

Some options for the future

There are several directions that might be taken in the future development of the welfare state, if politicians wished to extend empowerment. The three outlined below by no means cover the full range.

One option would be for governments to press on with a notion of need and empowerment linked - as in the 1980s - with heavy reliance on individual consumer choice in market settings. While not necessarily universalistic in terms of all people having similar access to services or resources, an economic liberal model does imply in principle an equivalence of status for all participants. This is because in theory markets do not distinguish between the money or labour offered by a black person or a white person, or that of a woman or a man. Consequently market arrangements do imply a kind of universality for those who can take part, even though this is rarely achieved fully in practice. We touched on this model for welfare provision in chapter 7, when we noted that minority ethnic communities have not benefited greatly through economic liberalism. Measures to empower marginalised consumers more fully within such a model might include strengthening anti-discrimination laws and agencies, and facilitating access to capital. Government could also strengthen the capacity of individual consumers to challenge suppliers of welfare by encouraging collective organization and representation of consumers or clients.

139

A *second option* was also touched on in chapter 7, when we noted that a stress on the individual need not rely only on markets, but can also depend on a variety of rights, including rights to welfare outside markets. We might assert that rights to the supply of services, monies or goods can shade into other welfare state rights, such as political and legal equalities; the one often requires reinforcing by the other in order to have full value. Thus access to services is closely affected by political, legal and social status, while one's capacity to operate in the political or legal spheres is heavily influenced by resources of a material kind. In any event, rights based approaches to welfare may take non market as well as market orientated forms. Some advocates of markets might suggest that the two could also be combined in certain circumstances; as for example in the idea of a universal system of education spending vouchers to which everyone would be entitled by right, to be spent in a market for educational services. It is sometimes argued that rights or entitlements to welfare might need to be 'constitutionally entrenched' in some way, but there are already forms of welfare right - although rarely conceived of in those terms - which have heavy constitutional or legal protection; rights of property. It would be feasible to incorporate certain property rights within a broader model of individualized welfare rights.

A *third option* would be for governments to encourage communitarian, locality based, and particularistic approaches to social policy. In one sense this is a potentially pluralistic route; it would mean acknowledging and accommodating diversity far more than at present, and retreating from the paternalism, centralism and economic liberalism that have dominated the UK welfare system. It would also be likely to emphasize collective forms of empowerment. There may be elements in experiences or debates in other countries that would be relevant to this (see for instance discussion in Spicker, 1993/94), but in Britain there is both an underdeveloped literature on collective empowerment and a lack of varied and lasting experience of it in practice. Consequently we have little clear idea of the principles or structures that would best sustain it, or of how to deal with the tensions it might create with individualism. The discussion that follows will explore some potential collective rights based approaches, and individual ones, and then consider possibilities of connecting them. We will argue that, if governments wished, it would not be too difficult to accommodate a larger measure of pluralism without sacrificing the claims of individuals to universalistic treatment. Interestingly, property rights - neglected by social democratic welfare writers - might have a significant role to play.

Groups and their rights claims; separatism and empowerment

Our material on housing has implied that an experience of exclusion is one of the motors that can drive or reinforce demands for particularism and separatism. Thus people who feel a shared sense of disadvantage may band together to resist discriminatory practices and to obtain a stronger say in events. Or people with a sense of obligation, leadership and duty within a community may make efforts to obtain resources and establish organizational structures to help those households that they feel are losing out. Attacks from racists on colour or culture may also influence the politics of identity, perhaps strengthening people's wish to value their own religious institutions and practices, their view of connections with histories and struggles outside the UK, or their notions of black political mobilization in Britain. Clearly there is no certainty that groups will find common cause with each other just because they share the experience of negative discrimination, and they may disagree or diverge. In the case of housing, however, a sense of communities being undervalued and deprived of resources has provided motivation for individual and collective action, and some measure of coherence and joint mobilization across organizations or communities. As we have also observed, the role of public agencies has been highly significant, encouraging specific organizational forms and objectives, but at the same time acknowledging to a degree the importance of previous exclusion and of cultural diversity.

In any event, particularism and separatism can reflect and take account of a variety of factors. This may be true of separatism as a strategy and of particularism as a type of practice. Separatism might have a number of different targets and meanings, depending on context, and be pursued either alongside or as an alternative to strategies seeking fuller integration. A key question will be about the relationship with universalistic values and goals. Thus we might ask how compatible are the ideas about benefiting a group, locality or religious community on the one hand, with notions of equality of status for individuals on the other? This can be asked in specific contexts like the debates over denominational education, where affirmation of a particular interpretation of culture or tradition might militate against equality of treatment for boys and girls (or against school employment for atheists, unmarried mothers, gay people or other 'less respectables'). Or it can raise issues at a broader level. Lloyd (1994), for example, discusses contradictions that arise in anti-racist movements, sometimes revolving around questions of identity or difference versus universalism, in an apparent dichotomy. This connects with our themes on the tensions between communitarianism and individualism. Community orientated approaches imply a measure of particularism, with an orientation to the needs of local residents, yet this prioritizes some people while leaving others outside. A

141

call for fuller recognition of 'difference' in the interests of a group or community can mean going down this road. We might consider how far the pursuit of 'difference' undermines demands for more equal treatment for individuals, and how far the two goals are mutually supporting.

This set of concerns mirrors some questions which may arise with broader programmes of 'positive discrimination' or 'positive action' formulated under the banners of anti-racism, anti-sexism or anti-disablism. An argument can be made that there is a need to compensate for past disadvantage and its present day consequences. This may require a programme of positive actions to assist disadvantaged groups; for example by prioritizing women, black people or disabled people for training or appointments to jobs. Clearly this is less about responding to cultural or locality differences than about broad cleavages running across society. In the UK this type of policy has not been carried very far, but in the USA there is more experience of such efforts. The debate need not be cast in the way we have discussed things above, in terms of communitarianism and localism, but instead can be seen as a matter of trying to prioritize one group or other across a general sphere of action such as access to education, jobs or contracts. Arguments in favour of positive action do not relate only to prospects for individuals, but to the need for black people in general to have more of a voice through senior positions, the need for more role models, and so forth. Nonetheless, tensions can arise, in particular in the conflicts between universality of treatment and the claims of the previously disadvantaged. There are a number of complications, not least because the beneficiaries of broad positive discrimination strategies sometimes might be the more privileged from amongst the disadvantaged groups (for some issues see Edwards, 1994). If relative economic need is not the central criterion, then perhaps prosperous white women or middle class black male professionals might be the most likely gainers, at the expense of people who are no better off than they are. In any event, a programme which overtly gives preference to one broad category at the expense of others can clearly be a challenge to conventional universality of status, just as a particularism based on locality or community can be. This does not necessarily invalidate such programmes, but makes them vulnerable to challenge. In the USA, recent events apparently suggest some backlash against preference programmes of this type; interestingly, press reports suggest a legal challenge has arisen over the award of building contracts to a minority ethnic firm despite submission of a lower tender from a white run company.[2]

Returning to the question about the compatibility of the pursuit of difference and the claims for equality, the answer may be that we need to look at very specific circumstances and experiences. In this book we can only deploy housing examples with any confidence, so our analysis need not apply to other territory.

Lloyd suggests that both 'differentialism/particularism' and universalism are 'the subjects of myth-making, a process whereby grand ideas are appropriated and reforged through reference to heroic struggles of the past' (Lloyd, 1994,p.223). In the case of UK housing struggles and mobilizations this appears relatively muted, since many activists are highly pragmatic. On the other hand there is often a very definite and understandable desire to prioritize housing specific kinds of households, and to affirm a shared cultural, political or religious standpoint. For example, one of the Muslim organizations contacted in northern England fieldwork in 1989/90 apparently introduced all its committee meetings in a religious manner. This was not without flexibility, however, since a white Christian clergyman who was a committee member was invited to say an opening prayer on an occasion when he seemed the most appropriate person present. For several community based housing associations the need to deal with or work alongside other agencies, and to connect with white allies, was perhaps an important factor. Interactions with the Housing Corporation, differing minority ethnic housing organizations, local authorities and white run housing associations might all have effects on the perceptions or strategies of minority ethnic activists. Committees often included white people thought likely to assist, or offering specific skills. Processes of incorporation of associations into official programmes could influence this, or the extent to which certain male dominated committees felt it necessary to include female participants. Conclusions to be drawn from housing research are that there is great diversity, that culture in the housing context is not some kind of fixed or uncontested variable, and that separatist organizational strategies do not necessarily imply an abandonment of universalistic values or a retreat from interaction. Interaction perhaps may encourage an awareness of equal opportunity questions, and consequently a heightened understanding of inequalities and demands for universal access to resources. On the other hand notions of community empowerment and separatism do have a number of significant implications of an exclusive nature in housing. The organizations do wish to give priority to particular categories of people, not just in terms of housing provision but also in jobs, and this can be viewed by activists as extending to the area of contract allocation in some instances. The targets might be to establish mechanisms for voluntary participation within distinct organizations controlled by minority ethnic people, new routes of access to services and consumption of material goods outside existing channels, jobs within the new organizations, and control of capital and its use. These goals imply a set of collective rights to housing opportunities, to jobs generated by social housing expenditure, and to property. The property dimension might also be conceived of in terms of the desire to facilitate owner-occupation for some client households (although this hope had been frustrated by financial barriers to shared ownership in the case study instances encountered at the time of the present writer's fieldwork).

Individuals and their rights claims; universalism

Collective or communitarian approaches with a separatist emphasis can be attacked on a number of grounds. Firstly, it can be argued that prospects for social integration or for excellence in service delivery can be undermined by any fragmentation produced by separatism. This view tends to assume that integration is desirable and that existing provision is capable of excellence without organizational separatism. Thus, universalistic services are held to be superior in outcomes to separatism. It is not so easy to argue this view in a situation where services have been dominated by white people, where racism has been substantial, and where cultural sensitivity has been lacking. Nonetheless there is a case for integration and for recognising advantages of scale and standardization (such as cost savings).

Secondly, there is a view that selective provision for minorities is vulnerable to resource cuts, stigmatization, and political attack. Thus universalism is superior politically as far as protecting minorities is concerned. This is a possibility implied earlier in the book. Such an assertion may well be sustainable in a number of service areas, and has implications for the potential long term strategies of minority groups.

A third line of criticism, however, is the main issue now, for it concerns individual rights. This has a bearing on the development of community based and separatist solutions in several ways. One way is through the issue of differential treatment for individuals as a result of exclusion. As noted before, particularism can mean prioritizing some consumers or potential beneficiaries at the expense of those left out, and thus running against the concept of equality for individuals. Some people would have a weaker right than others to enjoy a service, an opportunity or facility. (As indicated above, this can arise also in the context of positive action programmes.) Such exclusion can have greatest impact in situations of resource shortage or rationing. Another way is through the differential treatment of individuals *within* a separatist setting. This connects with accountability and representativeness of an organization as well as with equality of treatment by it. Some potential beneficiaries might feel their individual rights were being undervalued by the organization which claimed to represent them or act for them. A further way of looking at the rights issue is to argue that individuals should not have their choices confined by being pre-allocated to some 'minority' category or other, and being expected to seek provision from a specific channel dedicated to that category.

All these arguments rest on the idea of individuals having rights to equality of status in some respect. This means a universalistic approach in which people's membership of a specific ethnic or other group would not outweigh the claims of people as individual citizens. Empowerment here is seen primarily as a matter of giving households and individuals rights to welfare and status.

Reconciling collective claims and individual rights; towards the 'empowering welfare state'?

A possible solution to some of these tensions, and to the problem of the vulnerability of selectivist approaches, may lie in a combination of the pluralistic with the universalistic. It seems probable that *a universalistic framework is needed for genuine pluralism to thrive*. This is partly a matter of equality of opportunities for individuals in legal and administrative terms, and partly a matter of a resources framework. It need not imply an extensive universalistic set of values and norms related to a traditional middle class white conception of appropriate lifestyles, behaviours and preferences. Universalistic rights claims will inevitably rest on some notion of shared standards and acceptable values, but perhaps one rooted more in widely supported liberties and opportunities than in the hegemony of powerful groups and interests. Access to resources is a key. To make space for a sustained and sensitive ethnic pluralism in housing it would be necessary to address some of the financial disadvantages facing households, and to develop a subsidy or incentives system geared not to maintaining tenures or providing a casualty service for the poorest, but to longer term household circumstances, the collective concerns of groups, and the strategies of households. To survive for long politically, a subsidy system would need to look acceptable to the majority, and would therefore require an element of self interest which would appeal widely. One possibility would be a universalistic type of housing allowance or credit, accessible in a variety of forms, both collective and individual (and including present owner-occupier subsidies in a reconstituted form). A universalistic approach of this kind need not preclude targeting of various sorts, and might contain opportunities for redressing inequalities. Thus it could be conceived of in terms of equality of status for individuals in relation to resource access frameworks rather than in terms of equal outcomes. With access to adequate resources, consumers could be enabled to choose the appropriate channels of provision, opting perhaps for collective forms of investment and management if they so wished. Some groups or local communities might aim to set aside the sometimes artificial boundary between housing work and social care and support services, building multi-purpose organizations from a specific religious or cultural starting point. Similarly, some communities might wish to activate the links between social housing investment and local economic regeneration, and use housing schemes to help small businesses or provide skills training for local residents. These possibilities would imply recognising collective action and self management as options which people were entitled to select, regardless of the preferences of economic liberalism and paternalism. Resources would be available in ways that permitted choice, rather than in ways which bound households to the paternalistic concerns of state agencies or to a notion of the isolated individual making a market style decision. None of this would rule out individual choice, since many consumers would operate on an individual basis, as they do now. A crucial factor would be that individuals would receive access to resources in ways that empowered them by creating rights in property in which they shared (or over which they exercised strong influence), not merely rights of use subject to bureaucratic gatekeeping.

This may all seem rather idealised, but the above sketch of possible arrangements is meant chiefly to illustrate the application of principles for combining individual universalized rights with the prospect of either collective or individual activity. We acknowledge that this is likely to be extremely difficult in situations of rationing and severe shortage.

We need to go further, however, and look at protection for individuals in the context of community/locality-based empowerment, in a society where housing inequalities are likely to remain very marked. Suppose that an organization wished to represent and assist a specific community, and exclude other people from its benefits - as a landlord or employer - on grounds of religion or ethnic origin. This would be negative discrimination of the kind frequently experienced by black people. We might find some grounds for a black run agency doing this via the concept of redressing a past imbalance in provision or representation, or responding to urgent needs brought about by racial harassment or discrimination; but even so there would need to be clear rules to govern the measurement of relative need amongst potential beneficiaries, the application of equal opportunities criteria to job applicants, etc. Especially in a situation of shortage of accommodation or work, there would need to be safeguards protecting the equality of status of applicants, and these safeguards could form part of a universalistic set of rights. Rules about administrative behaviour and the exercise of discretionary power would be required. In many ways these kinds of rules are already familiar to people in the housing association movement, and help constitute best practice. Beyond them, there is frequently a need to ensure a measure of democracy and openness to challenge in collective organizations receiving public funds or other support. This also requires a system of individual rights claims; in some settings underpinned by property rights (either shared or held individually).

The issue of the indirect benefits from housing investment seems at first glance a much more difficult topic. Any prioritizing of the award of building contracts on the basis of 'race', disability, religion, gender or geographical locality would face a host of objections. Economic liberalism is strongly opposed to positive actions along these lines, since free competition is thereby downgraded in favour of particularism. At the same time egalitarians could argue that any individual ought to have the right to apply for the work, provided his or her firm meets relevant criteria in terms of competence and integrity. This would be a question of universalistic rights to equivalent formal status. Even in this difficult instance, however, it would be possible to reconcile universalism with a community orientated approach. Instead of focussing directly and selectively on defined categories of individual beneficiaries or participants, subsidy could be linked with general performance measures which helped the locality. While no precise blueprint can be drawn up, there would undoubtedly be some mileage in adapting 'value for money' investment criteria to incorporate various facets of community development gain, particularly where prior disadvantage could be proven for an area or group (see concluding section of chapter 6). This would mean creating subsidy systems that rewarded (and gave a competitive advantage to) participants and schemes that could demonstrate clear gains beyond the provision of the housing tenancies. This could effectively encourage locally based firms and tradespeople, and any outside companies willing to work with the local community, subcontractors, suppliers, etc. At the same time, such an approach would preserve the equivalence of status of potential bidders. The definition of their capacity and relevant skills would have been broadened, to take account of a redefinition of desirable objectives for investment. It would be difficult for critics to condemn such a programme as one which could only benefit black people, and designed to exclude 'efficient' firms from competing. None of this would necessarily preclude various more conventional 'contract compliance' requirements, but we have shown how the debate about 'local labour' and so forth could be broadened. It does appear possible to prioritize without necessarily sacrificing certain kinds of equality of status amongst potential participants, and to retain some kinds of universality.

Concluding observations

Welfare states change in the face of a variety of pressures, and challenges from the grass roots are only one source of innovation. Nonetheless, our study has been able to say a number of things about the UK welfare state by looking at social movements and tensions over policy in the context of grass roots experience and pressure. 'Race' cannot be included in an overview without acknowledging its distinctiveness as an issue, but much can be learned for a general analysis by tackling policy development related to minority ethnic groups. We have been able to explore broad questions about the balance between communitarian, locality, and particularist interests on the one hand, and individual rights and universalistic strategies on the other. While it will not always be easy to strike a balance between these things, there may be ways of creating a genuinely more pluralistic welfare system without sacrificing the claims of individualism or the optimisms of universalism.

Notes

1. For an interesting discussion of universalism, difference and anti-racism see Lloyd, 1994. An example of a struggle relevant to cultural identity and particularism is the battle for Muslim schools; see Dwyer, 1993, and Cumper, 1990.
2. Relevant UK press reports include Freedland, 1995; The Guardian, 12 October, 1994; 2 March, 1995 (New York Times extract); 11 March, 1995.

Bibliography

Aboriginal and Torres Strait Islander Commission (1992), *ATSIC Annual Report 1990-91*, Australian Government Publishing Service, Canberra.

Aldridge, M. and Brotherton, C. (1987), 'Being a programme authority: Is it worthwhile?', *Journal of Social Policy*, 16,3, July, pp.349-69.

Ambrose, P. (1986), *Whatever Happened to Planning?*, Methuen, London.

Anderson, B. (1993), *Britain's Secret Slaves*, Anti-Slavery International and Kalayaan, London.

Arnstein, S. (1969), 'A ladder of citizen participation', *Journal of the American Institute of Planners*, XXXV, 4, July, pp.216-24.

Athar, M. (undated), *Asian Special Housing Initiative Agency: The Evidence: Survey of the Asian Community's Housing Needs*, Asian Special Housing Initiative Agency, Rochdale.

Atkinson, R. and Moon, G. (1994), *Urban Policy in Britain*, Macmillan, Basingstoke.

Bagguley, P. and Mann, K. (1992), 'Idle Thieving Bastards? Scholarly Representations of the "Underclass"', *Work, Employment and Society*, 6,1, March, pp.113-26.

Baistow, K. (1994/95), 'Liberation and regulation? Some paradoxes of empowerment', *Critical Social Policy*, 42;14,3, Winter 1994/95, pp.34-46.

Ball, H. (1988), 'The limits of influence: ethnic minorities and the Partnership Programme', *New Community*, 15,1, October, pp.7-22.

Barnes, C. (forthcoming), 'The Origins of Disability in Western Society', *unpublished paper*, 1994 draft, School of Sociology and Social Policy, University of Leeds, Leeds.

Baylies, C., Law, I. and Mercer, G. (eds), (1993), *The Nature of Care in a Multi-Racial Community*, Summary Report of an Investigation of the Support for Black And Ethnic Minority Persons after Discharge from Psychiatric Hospitals in Bradford and Leeds, Sociology and Social Policy Research

Working Paper 8, School of Sociology and Social Policy, University of Leeds, Leeds.

Bean, P. (1983), 'Utilitarianism and the welfare state' in Bean, P. and MacPherson, S. (eds), *Approaches to Welfare*, Routledge and Kegan Paul, London.

Begum, N., (1992), *Something to be proud of: The Lives of Asian Disabled People and Carers in Waltham Forest*, Waltham Forest Race Relations Unit and Disability Unit, Walthamstow.

Ben-Tovim, G., Gabriel, J., Law, I. and Stredder, K. (1986), 'A political analysis of local struggles for racial equality' in Rex, J. and Mason, D. (eds), *Theories of Race and Ethnic Relations*, Cambridge University Press, Cambridge.

Black Housing (1989), 'Black People and Homelessness', *Black Housing*, 5,11, December, pp.5-8.

Black Housing (1992), 'Focus on racial harassment' issue, *Black Housing*, 7,12, January.

Black Housing (1994), 'Housing Allocation in Oldham', *Black Housing*, 9,9, December 1993/January 1994, pp.8-10.

Bowles, S. and Gintis, H. (1986), *Democracy and Capitalism*, Routledge and Kegan Paul, London.

Bramley, G., Le Grand, J. and Low, W. (1989), 'How far is the poll tax a "community charge"? The implications of service usage evidence', *Policy and Politics*, 17,3, July, pp.187-205.

Briggs, A. (1963), *Victorian Cities*, Odhams Press, London.

Brown, C. (1984), *Black and White Britain: the third PSI survey*, Policy Studies Institute and Heinemann, London.

Brown, C. (1992), '"Same difference": the persistence of racial disadvantage in the British employment market' in Braham, P., Rattansi, A. and Skellington, R. (eds), *Racism and Antiracism*, Sage with The Open University, London.

Bulgin, S. (1995), 'Black architects fighting for a better deal', *Black Housing*, 10,6, January/February, pp.14-16.

Bulpitt, J. (1986), 'Continuity, Autonomy and Peripheralisation: the Anatomy of the Centre's Race Statecraft in England' in Layton-Henry, Z. and Rich, P.(eds), *Race, Government and Politics in Britain*, Macmillan,Basingstoke.

Burney, E. (1967), *Housing on Trial*, Institute of Race Relations and Oxford University Press, London.

Burrows, R. and Loader, B.(eds), (1994), *Towards a Post-Fordist Welfare State?*, Routledge, London.

Cabinet Office (1988), *Action For Cities*, Cabinet Office, London.

Cairncross, L., Clapham, D. and Goodlad, R. (1993), 'The Social Bases of Tenant Organisation', *Housing Studies*, 8,3, July, pp.179-93.

Cameron, C. and Soares, T. (1991), 'Value For Money', *Black Housing*, 7,2, March, pp.8-11.

Carlen, P. (1994), 'The governance of homelessness: legality, lore and lexicon in the agency-maintenance of youth homelessness', *Critical Social Policy*, 41;14,2, Autumn, pp.18-35.

Carter, M. and Ginsburg, N. (1994), 'New government housing policies', *Critical Social Policy*, 41,14,2, Autumn, pp.100-108.

Cater, J. (1981), 'The impact of Asian estate agents on patterns of ethnic residence: a case study in Bradford' in Jackson, P. and Smith, S. (eds), *Social Interaction and Ethnic Segregation*, Institute of British Geographers Special Publication 12, Academic Press, London.

Central Statistical Office (1993), *Social Trends* 23, 1993 edition, editor Rose, P., HMSO, London.

Champion, T. and Dorling, D. (1993), '1991 Census figures by tenure and ethnic group', *Housing Review*, 42,4, July/August, p.66.

Chancellor of the Exchequer, HM Treasury (1984), *Building Societies: A New Framework*, Cmnd.9316, HMSO, London.

Clapham, D. (1993), 'Tenant participation and the restructuring of public rented housing' in Williams, P. (ed.), *Management and Change in Social Housing*, Centre for Housing Management and Development, Papers in Housing Research 4, Department of City and Regional Planning, University of Wales College of Cardiff, Cardiff.

Clapham, D., Kemp, P. and Smith, S. (1990), *Housing and Social Policy*, Macmillan, Basingstoke.

Clapham, D. and Kintrea, K. (1992), *Housing Co-operatives in Britain; Achievements and prospects*, Longman, Harlow.

Cochrane, A. (1993), *Whatever Happened to Local Government?*, Open University Press, Buckingham.

Cole, I. and Furbey, R. (1994), *The Eclipse of Council Housing*, Routledge, London.

Coleman, B. (1973), *The idea of the city in nineteenth-century Britain*, Routledge and Kegan Paul, London.

Coleman, D. (1991), 'Government and the Housing Associations: a doomed romance?', *Housing Review*, 40,4, July/August, pp.79-80.

Commission for Racial Equality (CRE), (1982), *The Allocation of Council Housing; with particular reference to work permit holders*, report of a formal investigation, CRE, London.

Commission for Racial Equality (CRE), (1983), *Collingwood Housing Association Ltd.*, report of a formal investigation, CRE, London.

Commission for Racial Equality (CRE), (1984), *Race and Council Housing in Hackney*, report of a formal investigation, CRE, London.

Commission for Racial Equality (CRE), (1984a), *Abbey National Building Society*, report of a formal investigation, CRE, London.

Commission for Racial Equality (CRE), (1984b), *Race and Housing in Liverpool: A research report*, CRE, London.

Commission for Racial Equality (CRE), (1985), *Walsall Metropolitan Borough Council; practices and policies of housing allocation*, report of a formal investigation, CRE, London.

Commission for Racial Equality (CRE), (1987), *Living in Terror: A report on racial violence and harassment in housing*, CRE, London.

Commission for Racial Equality (CRE), (1988), *Homelessness and Discrimination*, report of a formal investigation, CRE, London.

Commission for Racial Equality (CRE), (1988a), *Racial Discrimination in a London Estate Agency*, report of a formal investigation, CRE, London.

Commission for Racial Equality (CRE), (1988b), *Learning in Terror*, CRE, London.

Commission for Racial Equality (CRE), (1990), *'Sorry it's gone'; testing for racial discrimination in the private rented housing sector*, CRE, London.

Commission for Racial Equality (CRE), (1990a), *Racial Discrimination in an Oldham Estate Agency*, report of a formal investigation, CRE, London.

Commission for Racial Equality (CRE), (1990b), *Putting Your House in Order; Estate Agents and Equal Opportunity Policies*, CRE, London.

Commission for Racial Equality (CRE), (1991), *Achieving Racial Equality in Housing Co-ops*, CRE, London.

Commission for Racial Equality (CRE), (1991a), *Code of Practice in Rented Housing*, CRE, London.

Commission for Racial Equality (CRE), (1993), *Housing Associations and Racial Equality*, CRE, London.

Community Relations Commission (1977), *Housing Choice and Ethnic Concentration*, Community Relations Commission, London.

Connolly, J. (1993), '"Level field" tilted against black HAs', *Voluntary Housing*, January, pp.14-15.

Cooke, P. (1989), 'Locality, Economic Restructuring and World Development' in Cooke, P. (ed.), *Localities*, Unwin Hyman, London.

Cooper, C. (1991), 'Tenant Participation in the 1990s', *Black Housing*, 7,11, December, pp.4-5.

Cooper, J. and Qureshi, T. (1993), 'Violence,Racial Harassment and Council Tenants: Reflections on the Limits of the Disputing Process', *Housing Studies*, 8,4, October, pp.241-55.

Cope, H. (1990), *Housing Associations: Policy and Practice*, Macmillan, Basingstoke.

Courtney, C. (1993), 'Rebuilding that turned to ruin', *The Guardian*, 3 December.

Cross, M. and Keith, M. (eds), (1993), *Racism, the City and the State*, Routledge, London.

Crouch, C. and Dore, R. (eds), (1990), *Corporatism and Accountability*, Clarendon Press, Oxford.

Cumper, P. (1990), 'Muslim schools: the implications of the Education Reform Act 1988', *New Community*, 16,3, April, pp.379-89.

Dalton, M. and Daghlian, S. (1989), *Race and Housing in Glasgow: the role of Housing Associations*, Commission for Racial Equality, London.

Damer, S. (1974), 'Wine Alley: The Sociology of a Dreadful Enclosure', *The Sociological Review*, New Series, 22,2,pp.221-48.

Davies, J.G. (1972), *The Evangelistic Bureaucrat*, Tavistock, London.

Deakin, N. (1995), 'Regenerating cities: means and ends' in Jones, H. and Lansley, J. (eds), *Social Policy and the City*, Avebury, Aldershot.

Dennis, N. (1970), *People and Planning*, Faber and Faber, London.

Department of the Environment (1988), *DoE Inner City Programmes 1987-88; A Report on Achievements and Developments*, Action For Cities, DoE, HMSO, London.

Department of the Environment and Welsh Office (1994), *The Housing (Right to Manage) Regulations 1994*, DoE Circular 6/94, WO Circular 21/94, London.

Dhillon-Kashyap, P. (1994), 'Black women and housing' in Gilroy, R. and Woods, R. (eds), *Housing Women*, Routledge, London.

Dixon, A. and Turkington, R. (1993), *Sheltered Housing in the West Midlands Metropolitan Area: The Experience of Caribbean and African Elders*, First Stage Report, Nehemiah Housing Association, Birmingham.

Doling, J. and Davies, M. (1983), 'Ethnic minorities and the protection of the Rent Acts', *New Community*, X,3, Spring, pp.487-92.

Donnison, D. and Middleton, A. (eds), (1987), *Regenerating the Inner City: Glasgow's Experience*, Routledge and Kegan Paul, London.

Doucet, M. and Weaver, J. (1991), *Housing the North American City*, McGill-Queen's University Press, Montreal.

Drakeford, M. (1993), 'But who will do the work?', *Critical Social Policy*, 38;13,2, Autumn, pp.64-76.

Drover, G. and Kerans, P. (eds), (1993), *New Approaches to Welfare Theory*, Edward Elgar, Aldershot.

Duke, C. (1970), *Colour and Rehousing: a study of Redevelopment in Leeds*, Institute of Race Relations, London.

Dunleavy, P. (1980), *Urban Political Analysis*, Macmillan, London.

Dworkin, R. (1981), 'Reverse Discrimination' in Braham, P., Rhodes, E. and Pearn, M. (eds), *Discrimination and Disadvantage in Employment: the Experience of Black Workers*, Harper and Row with The Open University Press, London.

Dwyer, C. (1993), 'Constructions of Muslim identity and the contesting of power: the debate over Muslim schools in the United Kingdom' in Jackson, P. and Penrose, J. (eds), *Constructions of race, place and nation*, UCL Press, London.

Eade, J. (1989), *The Politics of Community*, Avebury, Aldershot.

Eade, J. (1991), 'The political construction of class and community: Bangladeshi political leadership in Tower Hamlets, East London' in Werbner, P. and Anwar, M., *Black and Ethnic Leaderships in Britain*, Routledge, London.

Edwards, J. (1989), 'Positive discrimination as a strategy against exclusion: the case of the inner cities', *Policy and Politics*, 17,1, January, pp.11-24.

Edwards, J. (1994), 'Group Rights v. Individual Rights: The Case of Race-Conscious Policies', *Journal of Social Policy*, 23,1, January, pp.55-70.

Edwards, J. and Batley, R. (1978), *The Politics of Positive Discrimination*, Tavistock, London.

Esping-Andersen, G. (1990), *The Three Worlds of Welfare Capitalism*, Polity Press and Basil Blackwell, Cambridge and Oxford.

Eversley, D. (1992), 'Urban disadvantage and racial minorities in the UK' in Cross, M. (ed.), *Ethnic minorities and industrial change in Europe and North America*, Cambridge University Press, Cambridge.

Federation of Black Housing Organisations (FBHO), (1989), Special Report on Positive Action, *Black Housing*, 5,7, August issue.

Federation of Black Housing Organisations (FBHO), (1990), 'Who Cares For Our Elders?', *Black Housing*, 6,6, July issue.

Federation of Black Housing Organisations (FBHO), (1993), *National Directory of Black Housing Organisations*, 2nd edition, FBHO, London.

Federation of Black Housing Organisations (FBHO), (1994), 'Severe under-representation of Black staff and committee members in Merseyside HAs', *Black Housing*, 10,4, July/September, p.27.

Federation of Black Housing Organisations and Merseyside Area Profile Group (FBHO and MAPG), (1987), *Race and Public Sector Housing; lessons from Liverpool*, FBHO and MAPG, Liverpool.

Fenton, M. and Collard, D. (1984), 'Do Coloured Tenants Pay More? Some Evidence' in Ward, R. (ed.), *Race and Residence in Britain: Approaches to Differential Treatment in Housing*, Monograph on Ethnic Relations, Economic and Social Research Council, London.

Field, F., Meacher, M. and Pond, C. (1977), *To Him Who Hath*, Penguin, Harmondsworth.

154

Flett, H. (1984), 'Dimensions of Inequality: Birmingham Council Housing Allocations' in Ward, R. (ed.), *Race and Residence in Britain: Approaches to Differential Treatment in Housing*, Monograph on Ethnic Relations, Economic and Social Research Council, London.

Flett, H. (1984a), 'Dispersal Policies in Council Housing: Arguments and Evidence' in Ward, R. (ed.), *Race and Residence in Britain: Approaches to Differential Treatment in Housing*, Monograph on Ethnic Relations, Economic and Social Research Council, London.

Forrest, R. and Murie, A. (1994), 'Home Ownership in Recession', *Housing Studies*, 9,1, January, pp.55-74.

Forrest, R., Murie, A. and Williams, P. (1990), *Home Ownership: Differentiation and fragmentation*, Unwin Hyman, London.

Fraser, R. (1993), 'CCT, council housing and black people', *Black Housing*, 9,1/2, February/March, p.14.

Freedland, J. (1995), 'The whitelash starts here', *The Guardian*, 13 January.

Gibson, M. and Langstaff, M. (1982), *An Introduction to Urban Renewal*, Hutchinson, London.

Gilroy, P. (1987), *There Ain't No Black in the Union Jack*, Hutchinson, London.

Gilroy, R. with Marvin, S. (1993), *Good Practice in Equal Opportunities*, Avebury, Aldershot.

Gilroy, R. and Woods, R. (eds), (1994), *Housing Women*, Routledge, London.

Ginsburg, N. (1988/89), 'Institutional racism and local authority housing', *Critical Social Policy*, 24;8,3, Winter, pp.4-19.

Ginsburg, N. (1989), 'Racial harassment policy and practice: the denial of citizenship', *Critical Social Policy*, 26;9,2, Autumn, pp.66-81.

Glazer, N. and Young, K. (eds), (1983), *Ethnic Pluralism and Public Policy: Achieving Equality in the United States and Britain*, Heinemann Educational, London.

Goering, J. (1993), 'Towards the Comparative Exploration of Public Housing Segregation in England and the United States', *Housing Studies*, 8,4, October, pp.256-73.

Gough, I. (1979), *The Political Economy of the Welfare State*, Macmillan, London.

Goulbourne, H. (ed.), (1990), *Black Politics in Britain*, Avebury, Aldershot.

Gregson, N. and Lowe, M. (1994), *Servicing the Middle Classes*, Routledge, London.

Grenier, P. (1994), 'ASRA makes its name', *Voluntary Housing*, July, pp.26-8.

Habeebullah, M. and Slater, D. (1990), *Equal Access; Asian access to council housing in Rochdale*, Research and Policy Paper 11, Community Development Foundation, London.

Hajimichael, M. (1988), *The Sting In The Tail: race and 'equal opportunity' in London housing associations*, The Black Caucus, London Race and Housing Research Unit, London.

Hale, D. (1992), 'Why these blocks to shared ownership?', *Voluntary Housing*, November,pp.28-29.

Hambleton, R. (1977), 'Policies for Areas', *Local Government Studies*, New Series, 3,2, April, pp.13-29.

Hamnett, C. and Randolph, B. (1992), 'Racial minorities in the London labour and housing markets: a longitudinal analysis, 1971-81' in Cross, M. (ed.), *Ethnic minorities and industrial change in Europe and North America*, Cambridge University Press, Cambridge.

Hancock, L. (undated), *'Recognising Resistance: the development of the Black Housing Association movement'*, unpublished paper.

Harloe, M. and Martens, M. (1990), *New Ideas for Housing: the experience of three countries*, Shelter, London.

Harrison, M. (ed.), (1984), *Corporatism and the Welfare State*, Gower, Aldershot.

Harrison, M. (1986), 'Consumption and urban theory: an alternative approach based on the social division of welfare', *International Journal of Urban and Regional Research*, 10,2, June, pp.232-42.

Harrison, M. (1987), 'Property rights, philosophies, and the justification of Planning Control' in Harrison, M. and Mordey, R. (eds), *Planning Control: Philosophies, Prospects and Practice*, Croom Helm, London.

Harrison, M. (1989), 'The Urban Programme, Monitoring and Ethnic Minorities', *Local Government Studies*, 15,4, July/August, pp.49-64.

Harrison, M. (1990), 'Welfare State struggles, consumption, and the politics of rights', *Capital and Class*, 42, Winter, pp.107-30.

Harrison, M. (1991), *Achievements and Options: Black and minority ethnic housing organisations in action*, Armley, Leeds.

Harrison, M. (1991a), 'Local Authorities and Black-led Housing Associations', *Local Government Studies*, 17,5, September/October, pp.1-8.

Harrison, M. (1992), 'Black-led housing organisations and the housing association movement', *New Community*, 18,3, April, pp.427-37.

Harrison, M. (1992a), *Housing association schemes targeted on black and minority ethnic communities: some issues of design, security and development*, Social Policy and Sociology Research Working Paper 5, Department of Social Policy and Sociology, University of Leeds, Leeds.

Harrison, M. (1992b), *Housing association case studies: working towards good practice on minority ethnic issues*, Social Policy and Sociology Research Working Paper 4, Department of Social Policy and Sociology, University of Leeds, Leeds.

Harrison, M. (1992c), *Housing associations and minority ethnic needs: some survey results*, Social Policy and Sociology Research Report, Department of Social Policy and Sociology, University of Leeds, Leeds.

Harrison, M. (1992d), *The new regional charitable trusts assisting black-run housing organisations: an overview*, Social Policy and Sociology Research Working Paper 2, Department of Social Policy and Sociology, University of Leeds, Leeds.

Harrison, M. (1993/94), 'The Black Voluntary Housing Movement: pioneering pluralistic social policy in a difficult climate', *Critical Social Policy*, 39; 13,3, Winter, pp.21-35.

Harrison, M. (1994), 'Housing Empowerment, Minority Ethnic Organisations, and Public Policy in the UK', *Canadian Journal of Urban Research*, 3,1, June, pp.29-39.

Harrison, M. and Davies, J. (forthcoming 1995), *Housing Associations and Minority Ethnic Contractors*, Joseph Rowntree Foundation, York.

Harrison, M. and Stevens, L. (1981), *Ethnic Minorities and the Availability of Mortgages*, Department of Social Policy and Administration Social Policy Research Monograph 5, University of Leeds, Leeds.

Harrison, M.and Stevens, L. (1982), 'An Assessment of the Performance of the Local Authorities/Building Societies Support Scheme in Leeds, 1975-79', *Urban Studies*, 19,1, February, pp.59-63.

Harrison, S. and Pollitt, C. (1994), *Controlling Health Professionals*, Open University Press, Buckingham.

Haughton, G. (1990), 'Targeting Jobs to Local People: the British Urban Policy Experience', *Urban Studies*, 27,2, April, pp.185-98.

Haughton, G. and Whitney, D. (1989), 'Equal Urban Partners ?', *The Planner*, 15 December, pp.9-11.

Hausner, V. and Robson, B. (1985), *Changing Cities; an introduction to the ESRC Inner Cities Research Programme*, Economic and Social Research Council, London.

Henderson, J. and Karn, V. (1984), 'Race, Class and the Allocation of Public Housing in Britain', *Urban Studies*, 21,2, May, pp.115-28.

Henderson, J. and Karn, V. (1987), *Race, Class and State Housing: Inequality and the Allocation of Public Housing in Britain*, Gower, Aldershot.

Hendessi, M. (1987), *Migrants - The Invisible Homeless: A report on migrants' housing needs and circumstances in London*, Migrant Services Unit, London Voluntary Services Council, London.

Higgins, J., Deakin, N., Edwards, J. and Wicks, M. (1983), *Government and Urban Poverty*, Basil Blackwell, Oxford.

Home Office (1988), *A Scrutiny of Grants under Section 11 of the Local Government Act 1966*, Final Report, London, December.

Home Office (1992), *Safer Cities; Progress Report 1991/1992*, Home Office Crime Prevention Unit, London.

Home Office (1994), *Race and the Criminal Justice System 1994*, CJA Section 95, Home Office, London.

Housing Corporation (1989), *'The Tenants' Guarantee'*, The Housing Corporation, London.

Housing Corporation (1991), *Black and Minority Ethnic Housing Associations. Housing Corporation Policy; a draft for consultation*, The Housing Corporation, London.

Housing Corporation (1991a), *Black and Minority Ethnic Housing Associations. Housing Corporation Statement*, The Housing Corporation, London.

Housing Corporation (1992), *An Independent Future: Black and Minority Ethnic Housing Association Strategy 1992-1996*, The Housing Corporation, London.

Housing Corporation (1994), *Black and Minority Ethnic Housing Association Strategy Review 1994*, The Housing Corporation, London.

Ingham, G. (1984), *Capitalism Divided? The City and industry in British social development*, Macmillan, Basingstoke.

Institute of Race Relations (1987), *Policing Against Black People*, IRR, London.

Jacobs, B. (1986), *Black politics and urban crisis in Britain*, Cambridge University Press, Cambridge.

Jacobs, B. (1992), *Fractured Cities: Capitalism, community and empowerment in Britain and America*, Routledge, London.

Jacobs, S. (1985), 'Race,empire and the welfare state: council housing and racism', *Critical Social Policy*, 13;5,1, Summer, pp.6-28.

Jeffers, S. (1991), 'Black Sections in the Labour Party: the end of ethnicity and "godfather" politics?' in Werbner, P. and Anwar, M., *Black and Ethnic Leaderships in Britain*, Routledge, London.

Jeffers, S. (1993), 'Is Race Really the Sign of the Times or is Postmodernism only skin deep?' in Cross, M. and Keith, M. (eds), *Racism, The City and The State*, Routledge, London.

Jenkins, R. (1992), 'Black workers in the labour market: the price of recession' in Braham, P., Rattansi, A. and Skellington, R. (eds), *Racism and Antiracism*, Sage with The Open University, London.

Jesson, J. (1990), 'Contract compliance in the construction industry: a comparative view', *New Community*, 17,1, October, pp.59-69.

Johnson, N. (1987), *The Welfare State in Transition*, Wheatsheaf, Brighton.

Johnson, T. (1982), 'The state and the professions: peculiarities of the British' in Giddens, A. and Mackenzie, G., *Social class and the division of labour*, Cambridge University Press, Cambridge.

Jones, A. (1994), *The Numbers Game: Black and minority ethnic elders and sheltered accommodation*, Anchor Housing Trust, Oxford.

Jones, H. and Lansley, J. (eds), (1995), *Social Policy and the City*, Avebury, Aldershot.

Joseph Rowntree Foundation (JRF), (1990), *Findings; Tenant Participation in Council Housing*, Housing Research 8, January, JRF, York.

Joseph Rowntree Foundation (JRF), (1990a), *Findings; The scope for self-help in housing construction and design*, Housing Research 11, June, JRF, York.

Joseph Rowntree Foundation (JRF), (1991), *Findings; Tenant participation in Wales*, Housing Research 46, September, JRF, York.

Joseph Rowntree Foundation (JRF), (1991a), *Findings; Disabled people and institutional discrimination*, Social Policy Research 21, November, JRF, York.

Joseph Rowntree Foundation (JRF), (1992), *Findings; Housing association response to the needs of minority ethnic communities*, Housing Research 55, March, JRF, York.

Joseph Rowntree Foundation (JRF), (1992a), *Findings; Housing association development after the 1988 Housing Act*, Housing Research 56, March, JRF, York.

Joseph Rowntree Foundation (JRF), (1992b), *Findings; The impact of the Housing Act 1988 on housing associations*, Housing Research 61, June, JRF, York.

Joseph Rowntree Foundation (JRF), (1992c), *Findings; The extent of negative equity*, Housing Research 69, November, JRF, York.

Joseph Rowntree Foundation (JRF), (1993), *Findings; Housing provision for refugees*, Housing Research 80, March, JRF, York.

Joseph Rowntree Foundation (JRF), (1993a), *Findings; New housing association estates: emerging problems*, Housing Research 84, April, JRF, York.

Joseph Rowntree Foundation (JRF), (1993b), *Findings; Urban regeneration: UK and German problems and approaches*, Housing Research 100, and Supplement, *Policy Options, Regenerating multiply-deprived neighbourhoods*, December, JRF, York.

Joseph Rowntree Foundation (JRF), (1993c), *Findings; The spread of negative equity*, Housing Research 101, December, JRF, York.

Joseph Rowntree Foundation (JRF), (1994), *Findings; A positive role for local government - lessons for Britain from other countries*, Local and Central Government Relations Research 29, July, JRF, York.

Joseph Rowntree Foundation (JRF), (1994a), *Findings; The governance gap: quangos and accountability*, Local and Central Government Relations Research 30, September, JRF, York.

Joseph Rowntree Foundation (JRF), (1994b), *Findings; Community involvement in City Challenge*, Housing Research 105, January, JRF, York.

159

Joseph Rowntree Foundation (JRF), (1994c), *Findings; The impact of higher rents*, Housing Research 109, March, JRF, York.

Joseph Rowntree Foundation (JRF), (1994d), *Findings; Investment in social housing to fall to lowest level in many decades*, Housing Research 112, June, JRF, York.

Joseph Rowntree Foundation (JRF), (1994e), *Findings; Housing association lettings to homeless people*, Housing Research 117, July, JRF, York.

Joseph Rowntree Foundation (JRF), (1994f), *Findings; Home owners in negative equity*, Housing Research 120, July, JRF, York.

Joseph Rowntree Foundation (JRF), (1994g), *Findings; Community participation and empowerment: putting theory into practice*, Housing Summary 4, August, JRF, York.

Julienne, L. (1994), 'Mergers, Group Structures and other relationships', *Black Housing*, 10,3, May/June, pp.19-20.

Karn, V., Kemeny, J. and Williams, P. (1985), *Home Ownership in the Inner City; Salvation or Despair?*, Gower, Aldershot.

Kearns, A. (1990), 'Housing Policy, Deprivation and Space: the case of stress areas', *Policy and Politics*, 18,2, April, pp.119-34.

Kearns, A. (1994), 'Getting it right on governance', *Voluntary Housing*, November, pp.8-10.

Kemeny, J. (1992), *Housing and social theory*, Routledge, London.

Kingston, M. (1992), 'From Housing Co-operative to Housing Association', *Black Housing*, 8,4, May, pp.8-9.

KPMG Management Consulting, for Aboriginal and Torres Strait Islander Commission (1994), *Review of the Aboriginal and Torres Strait Islander Housing Organisations*, Data Collection Project, ATSIC, Woden, ACT, Australia.

Lawless, P. (1989), *Britain's Inner Cities*, 2nd edition, Paul Chapman, London.

Leather, P. and Mackintosh, S., (1993), 'Housing renewal in an era of mass home ownership' in Malpass, P. and Means, R. (eds), *Implementing Housing Policy*, Open University Press, Buckingham.

Le Grand, J. (1982), *The Strategy of Equality*, George Allen and Unwin, London.

Leigh, W. (1991), 'Civil Rights Legislation and the Housing Status of Black Americans: An overview', 'Trends in the Housing Status of Black Americans across selected Metropolitan Areas', and 'Glossary: Federal Housing Subsidy Programs', *The Review of Black Political Economy*, 19,3-4, Winter/Spring, pp.5-28,43-64,241-53.

Lemos Associates (1994), *Black Housing Associations in London*, Lemos Associates,London.

Lipsky, M. (1980), *Street-Level Bureaucracy*, Russell Sage Foundation, New York.

Lister, R. (1991), 'Citizenship engendered', *Critical Social Policy*, 32;11,2, Autumn, pp.65-71.

Lister, R. (1993), 'Tracing the contours of women's citizenship', *Policy and Politics*, 21,1, January, pp.3-16.

Little, J. (1994), *Gender, Planning and the Policy Process*, Pergamon, Oxford.

Llewelyn-Davies, H. (1995), 'Women's places', *Roof*, 20,1, January/February, p.36.

Lloyd, C. (1994), 'Universalism and Difference: The Crisis of Anti-Racism in the UK and France' in Rattansi, A. and Westwood, S. (eds), *Racism, Modernity and Identity*, Polity Press and Blackwell, Cambridge and Oxford.

London Race and Housing Forum (1981), *Racial Harassment on Local Authority Housing Estates*, CRE, London.

Love,A-M. and Kirby, K. (1994), *Racial Incidents in Council Housing: The Local Authority Response*, Department of the Environment, HMSO, London.

Lush, P. and Beeby, M. (1993), 'Black staff are getting a rough deal in white housing associations', *Black Housing*, 9,8, September/November, pp.12-14.

Lustiger-Thaler, H. and Shragge, E. (1993), 'Social Movements and Social Welfare: The Political Problem of Needs' in Drover, G. and Kerans, P. (eds), *New Approaches to Welfare Theory*, Edward Elgar, Aldershot.

McArthur, A. (1995), 'The active involvement of local residents in strategic community partnerships', *Policy and Politics*, 23,1, January, pp.61-71.

McKay, D. (1977), *Housing and Race in Industrial Society*, Croom Helm, London.

McKie, R. (1971), *Housing and the Whitehall Bulldozer*, Hobart Paper 52, Institute of Economic Affairs, London.

Macnicol, J. (1987), 'In Pursuit of the Underclass', *Journal of Social Policy*, 16,3, July, pp.293-318.

Malpass, P. (1993), 'Housing Management - By the People for the People', *Housing Review*, 42,4, July/August, pp.58-61.

Malpass, P. and Means, R. (eds), (1993), *Implementing Housing Policy*, Open University Press, Buckingham.

Malpass, P. and Murie, A. (1994), *Housing Policy and Practice*, 4th edition, Macmillan, Basingstoke.

Mama, A. (1989), *The Hidden Struggle*, London Race and Housing Research Unit, London.

Mann, K. (1992), *The Making of an English 'Underclass'?*, Open University Press, Milton Keynes.

Memon, A. (1988), 'Voluntary organizations and ethnic minority business development in inner cities: a comment', *Regional Studies*, 22,2, pp.155-60.

161

Miles, R. (1989), *Racism*, Routledge, London.

Misra, A. (1990), 'HNI: Black HAs Lose Out', *Black Housing*, 7,7, August, pp.12-13.

Misra, A. (1990a), *Supporting Black Housing Associations: a practical strategy*, National Federation of Housing Associations, London.

Misra, A. (1991), *Stock transfers to black housing associations: a guide for both transferring and black housing associations*, National Federation of Housing Associations, London.

Moore, R. (1992), 'Labour and housing markets in inner city regeneration', *New Community*, 18,3, April, pp.371-86.

Moore, R. (1995), 'Urban policy: problems and paradoxes' in Jones, H. and Lansley, J., *Social Policy and the City*, Avebury, Aldershot.

Mullins, D. (1992), 'From local politics to state regulation: the legislation and policy on race equality in housing', *New Community*, 18,3, April, pp.401-13.

Mullings, B. (1991), *The Colour of Money*, London Race and Housing Research Unit, London.

Mullings, B. (1992), 'Investing in public housing and racial discrimination: implications in the 1990s', *New Community*, 18,3, April, pp.415-25.

Munt, I. (1994), 'Race, urban policy and urban problems: a critique on current UK practice' in Thomas, H. and Krishnarayan, V. (eds), *Race Equality and Planning*, Avebury, Aldershot.

Murie, A. (1991), 'Government and the Social Rented Sector: A rejoinder to David Coleman', *Housing Review*, 40,6, November/December, pp.115-18.

National Federation of Housing Associations (NFHA), (1988), *Building your future: self build housing initiatives for the unemployed*, NFHA, London.

Niner, P. (1975), *Local Authority Housing Policy and Practice*, Occasional Paper 31, Centre for Urban and Regional Studies, University of Birmingham, Birmingham.

Niner, P. (1984), 'Housing associations and ethnic minorities', *New Community*, 11,3, Spring, pp.238-48.

Niner, P. (1987), 'Housing associations and Ethnic Minorities' in Smith, S. and Mercer, J. (eds), *New Perspectives on Race and Housing in Britain*, Centre for Housing Research, University of Glasgow, Glasgow.

Nother, P. (1994), 'Issues of governance', *Voluntary Housing*, July, pp.10-12.

Nother, P. (1994a), 'Step Forward Ujima', *Housing Associations Weekly*, 390,2 December, pp.14-16.

Oke, L. (1993), 'A black and white success story', *Voluntary Housing*, September, pp.22-3.

Oliver, M. and Zarb, G. (1989), 'The Politics of Disability: a new approach', *Disability, Handicap and Society*, 4,3, September, pp.221-39.

Owen, D. (1992), *Ethnic Minorities in Great Britain; Settlement Patterns*, 1991 Census Statistical Paper 1, National Ethnic Minority Data Archive, Centre for Research in Ethnic Relations, University of Warwick, Warwick.

Owen, D. (1993), *Ethnic Minorities in Great Britain; Age and gender structure*, 1991 Census Statistical Paper 2, National Ethnic Minority Data Archive, Centre for Research in Ethnic Relations, University of Warwick, Warwick.

Owen, D. (1993a), *Ethnic Minorities in Great Britain; Housing and family characteristics*, 1991 Census Statistical Paper 4, National Ethnic Minority Data Archive, Centre for Research in Ethnic Relations, University of Warwick, Warwick.

Patel, A. (1987), 'The Housing Needs of Elderly Asians', *Housing Review*, 36,3, May/June, pp.90-1.

Peach, C. and Byron, M. (1994), 'Council House Sales, Residualisation and Afro Caribbean Tenants', *Journal of Social Policy*, 23,3, July, pp.363-83.

Penoyre and Prasad Architects, with Audley English Associates, Matrix Feminist Architectural Co-op, Elsie Owusu Architects, and Safe Neighbourhoods Unit (1993), *Accommodating Diversity; The design of housing for minority ethnic, religious and cultural groups*, National Federation of Housing Associations and North Housing Trust, London.

Phillips, D. (1981), 'The social and spatial segregation of Asians in Leicester' in Jackson, P. and Smith, S. (eds), *Social Interaction and Ethnic Segregation*, Institute of British Geographers Special Publication 12, Academic Press, London.

Phillips, D. (1986), *What price equality?*, GLC Housing Research and Policy Report 9, Greater London Council, London.

Phillips, D. and Karn, V. (1992), 'Race and housing in a property owning democracy', *New Community*, 18,3, April, pp.355-369.

Pinsky, B. and D'Sousa, M. (1988), *Catalogue of Canadian Housing and Shelter Organizations*, Rooftops Canada Foundation, Toronto.

Pinto, R. (1993), *The Estate Action Initiative*, Avebury, Aldershot.

Poulter, S. (1986), *English Law and Ethnic Minority Customs*, Butterworths, London.

Prairie Research Associates (1991), *Tenant Organizations in Canada; Six site studies*, PRA, Winnipeg.

Prairie Research Associates (1991a), *The Relationship between Newcomer Tenants and their Landlords*, Lawrence Whytehead, Manitoba Interfaith Immigration Council.

Public Sector Management Research Unit, Aston University, (1985), *Five Year Review of the Birmingham Inner City Partnership*, Department of the Environment, London.

Ramdin, R. (1987), *The Making of the Black Working Class in Britain*, Gower, Aldershot.

Randall, B. (1994), 'Serving the black housing movement', *Voluntary Housing*, September, pp.70-71.

Randall, S. (1991), 'Local government and equal opportunities in the 1990s', *Critical Social Policy*, 31;11,1, Summer, pp.38-58.

Randolph, B. (1993), 'The re-privatization of housing associations' in Malpass, P. and Means, R. (eds), *Implementing Housing Policy*, Open University Press, Buckingham.

Rao, N. (1990), *Black Women in Public Housing*, Black Women in Housing Group, London Race and Housing Research Unit, London.

Ratcliffe, P. (1992), 'Renewal, regeneration and "race": Issues in urban policy', *New Community*, 18,3, April, pp.387-400.

Rattansi, A. (1994), '"Western" Racisms, Ethnicities and Identities in a "Postmodern" Frame' in Rattansi, A. and Westwood, S. (eds), *Racism, Modernity and Identity*, Polity Press and Blackwell, Cambridge and Oxford.

Rattansi, A. and Westwood, S. (eds), (1994), *Racism, Modernity and Identity*, Polity Press and Blackwell, Cambridge and Oxford.

Rattansi, A. and Westwood, S. (1994a), 'Modern Racisms, Racialized Identities' in Rattansi, A. and Westwood, S. (eds), *Racism, Modernity and Identity*, Polity Press and Blackwell, Cambridge and Oxford.

Redman, P. (1992), *Moving Targets*, Leeds Federated Housing Association, Leeds.

Rex, J. (1986), *Race and Ethnicity*, Open University Press, Milton Keynes.

Rex, J., Joly, D. and Wilpert, C. (eds), (1987), *Immigrant Associations in Europe*, Gower, Aldershot.

Rex, J. and Mason, D. (eds), (1986), *Theories of Race and Ethnic Relations*, Cambridge University Press, Cambridge.

Rex, J. and Moore, R. (1967), *Race, Community and Conflict*, Institute of Race Relations and Oxford University Press, London.

Rex, J. and Tomlinson, S. (1979), *Colonial immigrants in a British city: A class analysis*, Routledge and Kegan Paul, London.

Rich, P. (1987), 'The Politics of Race and Segregation in British Cities with reference to Birmingham 1945-1976' in Smith, S. and Mercer, J. (eds), *New Perspectives on Race and Housing in Britain*, Centre for Housing Research Studies in Housing 2, University of Glasgow, Glasgow.

Robson, B., Bradford, M., Deas, I., Hall, E., Harrison, E., Parkinson, M., Evans, R., Garside, P., Harding, A. and Robinson, F. (1994), *Assessing The Impact of Urban Policy*, Department of the Environment, HMSO, London.

Rose, H. (1981), 'Rereading Titmuss: The Sexual Division of Welfare', *Journal of Social Policy*, 10,4, October, pp.477-501.

Saggar, S. (1993), 'The politics of "race policy" in Britain', *Critical Social Policy*, 37;13,1, Summer, pp.32-51.

Salami, A. (1991), 'First Black Contractors Conference in Liverpool', *Black Housing*, 7,6/7, July/August, p.4.

Sarre, P., Phillips, D. and Skellington, R. (1989), *Ethnic Minority Housing: Explanations and Policies*, Avebury, Aldershot.

Saunders, P. (1986), *Social Theory and the Urban Question*, Second edition, Hutchinson Education, London.

Saunders, P. (1990), *A Nation of Home Owners*, Unwin Hyman, London.

Savage, M., Barlow, J., Dickens, P. and Fielding, T. (1992), *Property, Bureaucracy and Culture*, Routledge, London.

Secretary of State for the Environment (1975), *Race Relations and Housing: Observations on the Report on Housing of the Select Committee on Race Relations and Immigration*, Cmnd.6232, HMSO, London.

Secretaries of State for the Environment, Scotland and Wales (1977), *Policy For The Inner Cities*, Cmnd.6845, HMSO, London.

Secretaries of State for the Environment and Wales (1987), *Housing: The Government's Proposals*, Cm.214, HMSO, London.

Shah, L. and Williams, P. (1992), *The Housing Needs of the Asian Elderly in Cardiff*, Research Report, Department of City and Regional Planning, University of Wales College of Cardiff, Cardiff.

Shakespeare, T. (1993), 'Disabled People's Self-organisation: a new social movement?', *Disability, Handicap and Society*, 8,3, September, pp.249-64.

Shaw, K. (1990), 'Ideology, control and the teaching profession', *Policy and Politics*, 18,4, October, pp.269-78.

Shiner, P. (1995), 'Making less seem more', *The Guardian*, 11 January, Society, 9.

Shukra, K. (1990), 'Black Sections in the Labour Party' in Goulbourne, H. (ed.), *Black Politics in Britain*, Avebury, Aldershot.

Sills, A., Taylor, G. and Golding, P. (1988), *The Politics of the Urban Crisis*, Hutchinson, London.

Simpson, A. (1981), *Stacking the Decks; A study of race, inequality and council housing in Nottingham*, Nottingham and District Community Relations Council, Nottingham.

Simpson, S. and Dorling, D. (1994), 'Those Missing Millions: Implications for Social Statistics of Non-response to the 1991 Census', *Journal of Social Policy*, 23,4, October, pp.543-67.

Sinfield, A. (1978), 'Analyses in the Social Division of Welfare', *Journal of Social Policy*, 7,2, April, pp.129-56.

Skocpol, T. (1991), 'Targeting within Universalism: Politically Viable Policies to Combat Poverty in the United States' in Jencks, C. and Peterson, P. (eds), *The Urban Underclass*, The Brookings Institution, Washington D.C.

Smith, D. (1977), *Racial Disadvantage in Britain*, Penguin, Harmondsworth.

Smith, S. (1989), *The Politics of 'Race' and Residence*, Polity Press and Basil Blackwell, Cambridge and Oxford.

Smith, S. with Hill, S. (1991), *'Race' and Housing in Britain: a review and research agenda*, report prepared for Joseph Rowntree Foundation 'Race' and Housing Workshop, April, York.

Soares, T. (1993), 'Third Degree Nominations', *Black Housing*, 8, 11/12, December 1992/January, p.7.

Solomos, J. (1988), *Black Youth, Racism and the State*, Cambridge University Press, Cambridge.

Solomos, J. (1991), 'The politics of race and housing', *Policy and Politics*, 19,3, July, pp.147-57.

Solomos, J. (1993), *Race and Racism in Britain*, 2nd edition, Macmillan, Basingstoke.

Solomos, J. and Back, L. (1991), *The Politics of Race and Social Change in Birmingham: Historical Patterns and Contemporary Trends*, Research Paper 1, Department of Politics and Sociology, Birkbeck College, London.

Solomos, J. and Back, L. (1994), 'Conceptualising racisms: social theory, politics and research', *Sociology*, 28,1, February, pp.143-61.

Solomos, J.,Findlay, B.,Jones, S. and Gilroy, P. (1982), 'The organic crisis of British capitalism and race: the experience of the seventies' in Centre For Contemporary Cultural Studies, *The Empire Strikes Back*, Hutchinson and CCCS, University of Birmingham, London.

Spicker, P. (1989), *Social Housing and the Social Services*, Institute of Housing and Longman, Coventry and Harlow.

Spicker, P. (1993/94), 'Understanding particularism', *Critical Social Policy*, 39;13,3, Winter, pp.5-20.

Stedman Jones, G. (1971), *Outcast London*, Clarendon Press, Oxford.

Stewart, M. (1987), 'Ten years of inner cities policy', *Town Planning Review*, 58,2, April, pp.129-45.

Stewart, M. (1994), 'Between Whitehall and Town Hall: the realignment of urban regeneration policy in England', *Policy and Politics*, 22,2, April, pp.133-45.

Stewart, M. and Whitting, G. (1983), *Ethnic Minorities and the Urban Programme*, School for Advanced Urban Studies Occasional Paper 9, University of Bristol, Bristol.

Taub, R. (1990), *Nuance and Meaning in Community Development: Finding Community and Development*, Community Development Research Center,

Graduate School of Management and Urban Policy, New School for Social Research, New York.

TEEGA Research Consultants (1983), *The Housing Situation of Canadian Immigrant Households*, Ottawa.

Thake, S.and Staubach, R. (1993), *Investing in people: Rescuing communities from the margin*, Joseph Rowntree Foundation with Anglo-German Foundation for the Study of Industrial Society, York.

Tickell, J. (1992), *America's Community Developers and the Empowerment Debate*, Report to The Commonwealth Foundation.

Titmuss, R. (1958), 'The Social Division of Welfare: Some Reflections on the Search for Equity' in Titmuss, R., *Essays on 'The Welfare State'*, Unwin University Books, London.

Todd, M. (1992), 'Slow train coming', *Roof*, 17,6, November/December, pp.16-17.

Todd, M. and Karn, V. (1993), 'Matters of Strategic Importance', *Inside Housing*, 23 July, pp.8-9.

Todd, M. and Karn, V. (1994), 'A Fatal Attraction ?', *Voluntary Housing*, October, pp.22-23.

Tomlins, R. (1994), 'Housing Associations and Race Equality', *Housing Review*, 43,2, March-April, pp.26-27.

Tucker, J. (1966), *Honourable Estates*, Victor Gollancz, London.

Ungerson, C. (1995), 'Gender, Cash and Informal Care: European Perspectives and Dilemmas', *Journal of Social Policy*, 24,1, January, pp.31-52.

Vaux, G.and Divine, D. (1988), 'Race and Poverty' in Becker, S. and MacPherson, S. (eds), *Public Issues Private Pain: Poverty, Social Work and Social Policy*, Insight, London.

Vidal, A. (1992), *Rebuilding Communities: A National Study of Urban Community Development Corporations*, Community Development Research Center, Graduate School of Management and Urban Policy, New School for Social Research, New York.

Wadhams, C. (1992), 'Outbreak of peace in inner cities?', *Roof*, 17,6, November/December, p.16.

Ward, C. (1974), *Tenants Take Over*, Architectural Press, London.

Werbner, P. and Anwar, M. (1991), *Black and Ethnic Leaderships in Britain*, Routledge, London.

Whitting, G. (1985), *Implementing An Inner City Policy*, School for Advanced Urban Studies Occasional Paper 22, University of Bristol, Bristol.

Wilkinson, M. (1993), 'British Tax Policy 1979-90: equity and efficiency', *Policy and Politics*, 21,3, July, pp.207-17.

Williams, B. and Lusk, P. (1993), *Helping Ourselves: tenant control and housing need*, National Federation of Housing Associations, Partners in Change, The Housing Corporation, London.

Williams, F. (ed.), (1977), *Why the Poor Pay More*, National Consumer Council, Macmillan, London.

Williams, F. (1989), *Social Policy: A Critical Introduction: Issues of Race, Gender and Class*, Polity with Blackwell, Cambridge and Oxford.

Williams, F. (1991), 'Somewhere over the rainbow: Universality and selectivity in social policy', Paper presented at *Social Policy Association conference*, Nottingham, July.

Williams, G. (1983), *Inner City Policy - A Partnership with the Voluntary Sector?*, NCVO Occasional Paper 3, Bedford Square Press, London.

Willmott, P. (ed.), (1994), *Urban Trends 2: A decade in Britain's deprived urban areas*, Policy Studies Institute, London.

Wilson, W. (1991), 'Studying inner-city social dislocations: the challenge of public agenda research', *American Sociological Review*, 56, February, pp.1-14.

Wrench, J., Brar, H. and Martin, P., with Johnson, M. (1993), *Invisible Minorities: racism in New Towns and New Contexts*, Centre for Research in Ethnic Relations, University of Warwick, Coventry.

Ye-Myint, C. (1992), *Who's Hiding: A report into 'non-priority homelessness' amongst people from black and ethnic communities in Tower Hamlets*, No Fixed Abode, London.

Young, K. and Mason, C. (eds), (1983), *Urban Economic Development*, Macmillan, London.